# STOTRĀÑJALIḤ

## Hymn Offerings

to

Śrī Rāmakṛṣṇa & the Holy Mother

By

Several Great Disciples

&

Devotees

Sanskrit Text

together with

transliteration and translation by

Swāmi Tapasyānanda

Śrī Rāmakṛṣṇa Math

16, Rāmakṛṣṇa Math Road

Mylapore, Madras 600 004.

Published by
© The President
Sri Ramakrishna Math
16, Ramakrishna Math Road,
Mylapore, Madras-600 004.


First Impression
I-3M 3C-3-1988

ISBN 81-7120-023-0

Printed in India at
Sri Ramakrishna Math Printing Press
Mylapore, Madras-600 004.

# Contents

# HYMN OFFERINGS

## Introduction

This small collection of Hymns is mainly meant for the daily use of aspirants devoted to Śrī Rāmakṛṣṇa and the Holy Mother, who are looked upon by many as the Divine Incarnation of the age and who therefore form the daily object of worship for them. After Japam and meditation the chanting of evocative hymns and praises enhances one's devotional fervour and gives a sense of completion to one's devotional practice.

The compositions included in this volume are mainly those of Swāmī Abhedānanda,* a direct disciple of Śrī Rāmakṛṣṇa and a great scholar and preacher. They are couched in simple but mellifluous Sanskrit in various attractive metres. All of them put together give a comprehensive resume of the events of the Master's life and message. Both the touch of fervent devotion and the literary beauty of the Sanskrit diction in which they are clothed, make these hymns of Swāmī Abhedānanda a very valuable and authoritative part of the devotional literature on Śrī Rāmakṛṣṇa and the Holy Mother.

*The Sanskrit Texts of the hymns by Swāmī Abhedānanda included herein are taken from 'Songs Divine' published by the Rāmakṛṣṇa Vedānta Math, 19-B, Raja Rajakrishna Street, Calcutta.

Besides Swāmī Abhedānanda's compositions, there is at the beginning, a Hymn by Swāmī Vivekānanda — a verse simple but pregnant with deep meaning. It was composed extempore by the Swāmī while consecrating a shrine of the Master in the newly built house of a devotee, Navagopāl Ghosh, at Rāmakṛṣṇa Puri, Howrah, on 6th February 1898. This verse has assumed great importance in the adoration of Śrī Rāmakṛṣṇa, as it forms a part of the Ārātrika Hymn wherever Śrī Rāmakṛṣṇa is worshipped.

Another important item in the collection is a Hymn by Swāmī Virajānanda in Tūṇika metre. Swami Virajānanda was an early disciple of the monastic Order and one of the most respected Presidents of the Śrī Rāmakṛṣṇa Math. He was one of those who had come into intimate contact with most of the direct disciples of Śrī Rāmakṛṣṇa from the days of Ālambazār Math, and therefore well-established in the traditions of the Order. His Hymn in the stirring Tūṇika metre forms an excellent channel for the expression of devotional sentiments.

Aṣṭottara-sata-nāmāvali by Swāmī Vimalānanda is another highly devotional and scholarly item included in this collection of hymns. Swāmī Vimalānanda was a great Sannyāsin noted for his scholarship in Sanskrit as also in philosophy, both eastern and western. His composition is noteworthy not only for its devotional fervour and appealing Sanskrit diction, but for the appropriateness and relevancy of all the expressions used. They help a devotee remember all the important incidents of Śrī Rāmakṛṣṇa's life and of his principal teachings. In fact it depicts Śrī Rāmakṛṣṇa's life as an embodiment of his teachings in the form of a praise with 108 expressions.

Besides the writings of the above-mentioned composers, there is also a praise of the Holy Mother in the form of a Sāradā-nāma-saṅkīrtanam by Swāmī Guṇātītānanda, suited for collective singing. It will be noticed that many of the expressions by which the Holy Mother is referred to in it, are not directly connected with her life and teachings, but are drawn from Paurāṇika depiction of the Devī in ancient texts. It therefore deals essentially with her divinity.

In addition to these verses on Śrī Rāmakṛṣṇa and the Holy Mother, we have included in this collection, two famous hymns — *the Stotra-ratna* and *the Gopikā-gītam*. These have been added both because of their extraordinary expression of devotional sentiments and because they help to increase the size of the volume with matter that is of general devotional appeal. About the scriptural contexts of these hymns and their subject matter, special Introductions are given at their beginning, in order to help readers who are not acquainted with the theological background of these hymns.

# SRĪ RĀMAKṚṢṆA STOTRAM
## By Swāmī Vivekānanda

*1*

ॐ ह्रीं ऋतं त्वमचलो गुणजित् गुणेड्यः
नक्तं दिवं सकरुणं तव पादपद्मम् ।
मोहङ्कषं बहुकृतं न भजे यतोऽहं
तस्मात्त्वमेव शरणं मम दीनबन्धो ॥

*Om Hrīṁ ṛtaṁ tvam acalo guṇajit guṇeḍyaḥ*
*naktam divaṁ sakaruṇaṁ tava pāda-padmam* |
*mohaṅ-kaṣaṁ bahu-kṛtaṁ na bhaje yato'haṁ*
*tasmāt tvam eva śaraṇaṁ mama dīna- bandho* ||

Thou art the Supreme Being indicated by the Bīja sounds Om and Hrīm.

Thou art the Truth immutable who art beyond the sway of Guṇas (Nature's modes), yet Thy glory do the Guṇas proclaim.

Day and night have I failed to worship Thy delusion-destroying feet with a longing heart and firm determination.

Therefore Thou art my sole refuge, O Friend of the lowly and the lost!

2

भक्तिर्भगश्च भजनं भवभेदकारि
गच्छन्त्यलं सुविपुलं गमनाय तत्त्वम् ।
वक्त्रोद्धृतोऽपि हृदये न च भाति किञ्चित्
तस्मात्त्वमेव शरणं मम दीनबन्धो ।।

*Bhaktir bhagaś ca bhajanaṁ bhava-bheda-kāri*
*gacchanty alam suvipulam gamanāya tattvam* |
*vaktrod-dhṛto'pi hṛdaye na ca bhāti kiñcit*
*tasmāt tvam eva śaraṇaṁ mama dīna-bandho* ||

Devotion, aspiration and worship—breakers of worldly bondage—are indeed sufficient to take one to the Supreme Truth.
While I talk much of these, my heart fails to reflect on them even in the least.
Therefore, Thou art my sole refuge, O Friend of the lowly and the lost!

3

तेजस्तरन्ति तरसा त्वयि तृप्ततृष्णाः
रागे कृते ऋतपथे त्वयि रामकृष्णे ।
मर्त्यामृतं तव पदं मरणोर्मिनाशं
तस्मात्त्वमेव शरणं मम दीनबन्धो ।।

*Tejastaranti tarasā tvayi tṛpta-tṛṣṇāḥ*
*rāge kṛte ṛta-pathe tvayi Rāmakṛṣṇe* |
*marty'āmṛtaṁ tava padaṁ maraṇormi-nāśam*
*tasmāt tvam eva śaraṇaṁ mama dīna-bandho* ||

Those who have found the fulfilment of all their desires in Thee
And developed loving attachment to Thee,
O Rāmakṛṣṇa, the apostle of truth and righteousness!
They do overcome very soon the heat of the passions of the heart.
Thy name is in sooth an immortal drink to Thy devotees, a veritable dispeller of the waves of death!
Therefore Thou art my sole refuge, O Friend of the lowly and the lost!

*4*

कृत्यं करोति कलुषं कुहकान्तकारि
ष्णान्तं शिवं सुविमलं तव नाम नाथ ।
यस्मादहं त्वशरणो जगदेकगम्य
तस्मात्त्वमेव शरणं मम दीनबन्धो ।।

*Kṛtyam karoti kaluṣaṁ kuhak'āntakāri*
*ṣṇāntaṁ śivaṁ suvimalaṁ tava nāma nātha|*
*Yasmād ahaṁ tv'aśaraṇo jagad-eka-gamya*
*tasmāt tvam eva śaraṇaṁ mama dīna-bandho||*

Lord, holy and sanctifying is Thy name ending with 'Ṣṇa', destroying delusion in all and transforming sinners into saints.
I am verily without any other shelter, O Thou, the goal of all the worlds!
Therefore Thou art my sole refuge, O Friend of the lowly and the lost!

5

स्थापकाय च धर्मस्य सर्वधर्मस्वरूपिणे
अवतारवरिष्ठाय रामकृष्णाय ते नमः ॥

*Sthāpakāya ca dharmasya sarva-dharma-svarūpiṇe |*
*avatāra-variṣṭhāya Rāmakṛṣṇāya te namaḥ ||*

O Rāmakṛṣṇa, founder of religion universal, and the embodiment of all world religions!
To Thee, the noblest of Divine Incarnations, I offer my salutation.

*Om namaḥ śrī bhagavate Rāmakṛṣṇāya namo namaḥ!*
*Om namaḥ śrī bhagavate Rāmakṛṣṇāya namo namaḥ!*
*Om namaḥ śrī bhagavate Rāmakṛṣṇāya namo namaḥ!*

# ŚRĪ RĀMAKṚṢṆA-LOKANĀTHA-STOTRAM

## By Swāmī Abhedānanda

*1*

लोकनाथश्चिदाकारो राजमानः स्वधामनि
कलिकल्मषमग्नानामुत्तारणचिकीर्षया ।
मायाशक्तिं समाश्रित्य योऽवतीर्णो महीतले
नमोऽस्तु रामकृष्णाय तस्मै श्रीगुरवे नमः ॥

*Loka-nāthaś cidākāro rājamānaḥ svadhāmani* |
*Kali-kalmaṣamagñānām uttāraṇa-cikīrṣayā* |
*Māyā-śaktiṁ samāśritya yo'vatīrṇo mahītale* |
*namo'stu Rāmakṛṣṇāya tasmai śrī-gurave namaḥ* ||

The Lord of the universe, of the nature of Pure Consciousness, ever resplendent in His transcendent majesty,
Being desirous of uplifting men grovelling in the ignorance that the baneful influence of the age of Kali has cast on them,
Did manifest as Rāmakṛṣṇa in this world, assuming His Power known as Māyā.
To Him Rāmakṛṣṇa, the World-Teacher, my obeisance.

2

सद्ब्राह्मणकुले जातो दिव्यदेहं समाश्रितः
बाल्ये यो दिव्यभावेन वयस्यैर्मुदमावहत् ।
विरक्तो यौवने तीव्रं मायापाश-विवर्जितः
नित्यमुक्तस्वभावोऽपि लोकानुग्रहकामतः ॥

*Sad-brāhmaṇa-kule jāto divya-dehaṁ samāśritaḥ |*
*bālye yo divyabhāvena vayasyair mudam āvahat |*
*virakto yauvane tīvraṁ māyāpāśa-vivarjitaḥ |*
*nitya-mukta-svabhāvo'pi lokānugraha-kāmataḥ ||*

Born in a family of pious Brāhmaṇas, with a body that was purely divine,
He spent His boyhood in the joyous company of comrades, though ever free and poised in the divine mood.
For promoting the world's welfare, He developed an intense spirit of renunciation in his youth,
Though he was by nature free and devoid of the bondage of Māyā.

3

लोकानामेव शिक्षार्थं तपस्तप्त्वा सुदुष्करम्
निद्राशनं परित्यज्य वर्षाणां द्व्यधिकान् दश ।
स्वस्वरूपं समाधाय सच्चिदानन्दविग्रहम्
दयामूर्त्तिः सदानन्दो जिज्ञासूनुपदिष्टवान् ।
तेषामज्ञाननाशाय लाभाय च परात्मनः
नमोऽस्तु रामकृष्णाय तस्मै श्रीगुरवे नमः ॥

*Lokānām eva śikṣārthaṁ tapas taptvā suduṣkaram |*
*nidrāśanam parityajya varṣāṇāṁ dva'dhikān daśa |*
*sva-svarūpaṁ samādhāya sat-cid-ānanda-vigraham |*
*dayā-mūrtiḥ sadānando jijñāsūn upadiṣṭavān ||*
*Teṣām ajñāna-nāśāya lābhāya ca parātmanaḥ |*
*namo 'stu Ramakṛṣṇāya tasmai śrī-gurave namaḥ |*

And to set an example to the world, he performed austerities, too difficult even to contemplate, abandoning sleep for a period of twelve years.
Then established in His own inherent nature constituted of Existence - Knowledge - Bliss,
He, a veritable embodiment of mercy and bliss, imparted instructions to aspirants
For the eradication of their ignorance and their attainment of the Supreme Atman.
To Him, Rāmakṛṣṇa, the World-Teacher, my salutation.

*4*

सत्यबोधतया साङ्गान् सर्वधर्मान् समाचरन्
धर्ममात्रन्तु सत्यं वै येन सम्यक् सुनिश्चितम् ।
नमोऽस्तु रामकृष्णाय तस्मै श्रीगुरवे नमः ॥

*Satya-bodhatayā sāṅgān sarva-dharmān samācaran |*
*dharma-mātraṁ tu satyam vai yena samyak suniścitam |*
*namo'stu Rāmakṛṣṇāya tasmai śrī-gurave namaḥ ||*

Having practised all religions and their auxiliaries with complete faith in their truth,
He arrived at the conviction that all of them were established in Truth.
To Him Rāmakṛṣṇa the World Teacher, my salutation.

*5*

यो भक्तान् भक्तिमार्गे तु निनाय लोकनायकः
आकृष्य मानसं तेषां भक्तिभावार्द्रया गिरा ।
दर्शयित्वा महाभावं परमानन्ददायकम्
नमोऽस्तु रामकृष्णाय तस्मै श्रीगुरवे नमः ॥

*Yo bhaktān bhakti-mārge tu nināya loka-nāyakaḥ* |
*ākṛṣya mānasaṁ teṣāṁ bhakti-bhāv'ārdrayā girā* |
*darśayitvā mahābhāvaṁ paramānanda-dāyakam* |
*namo'stu Rāmakṛṣṇāya tasmai śrī-gurave namaḥ* ||

He, the Lord of all, directed devotees along the path of devotion,
Having attracted them by words soaked in devotion,
And revealing to them His blissful state of Mahābhāva.
To Him Rāmakṛṣṇa the World Teacher, my obeisance.

*6*

ज्ञानिनो ज्ञानमार्गे च येन सम्यक् प्रवर्तितः ।
नमोऽस्तु रामकृष्णाय तस्मै श्रीगुरवे नमः ॥

*Jñānino jñāna-marge ca yena samyak pravartitaḥ* |
*namo'stu Rāmakṛṣṇāya tasmai śrī-gurave namaḥ* |

He by whom the seekers of knowledge were set on the path of knowledge,
To that Rāmakṛṣṇa the World-Teacher, my salutation.

7

यैर्मतैर्धार्मिका यस्मिन् धर्ममार्गे व्यवस्थिताः
तेषां तन्मतमादृत्य भक्तिस्तत्र दृढीकृता ।
प्रोत्साहिता यथान्यायं येन तत्साधनेष्वपि
नमोऽस्तु रामकृष्णाय तस्मै श्रीगुरवे नमः ॥

*Yair-matair-dhārmikā yasmin dharma-mārge vyavasthitāḥ* |
*teṣāṁ tan-matam ādṛtya bhaktis tatra dṛḍhīkṛtā* |
*pro'tsāhitā yathānyāyam yena tat sādhaneṣu'api* |
*namo'stu Rāmakṛṣṇāya tasmai śrī-gurave namaḥ* ||

Through whatever spiritual traditions Truth-seekers were found to strive,
He strengthened their faith in the same by his reverential attitude to such faiths,
And thus enthused them to strive along the paths of discipline as handed down by their traditions.
To him the World-Teacher Rāmakṛṣṇa, my salutation.

8

पूजिता येन वै शश्वत् सर्वेऽपि साम्प्रदायिकाः
सम्प्रदायविहीनो यः सम्प्रदायं न निन्दति ।
नमोऽस्तु रामकृष्णाय तस्मै श्रीगुरवे नमः ।

*Pūjitā yena vai śaśvat sarve'pi sāmpradāyikāḥ* |
*sampradāya vihīno yaḥ sampradāyam na nindati* |
*namo'stu Rāmakṛṣṇāya tasmai śrī-gurave namaḥ* ||

By him the followers of all sects were honoured and none criticised,
But himself was without any sect exclusively his own,
To that World-Teacher Rāmakṛṣṇa, my salutation.

*9*

शश्वल्लीलाविलासेन येन विश्वमिदं ततम् ।
लीलारूपं सदानन्दं रामकृष्णं नमाम्यहम् ॥

*Śaśval līlā-vilāsena yena viśvam idam tatam* |
*lilārūpaṁ sad'ānandaṁ Rāmakṛṣṇaṁ namāmy aham* ||

By whom this whole universe is pervaded in His sportive manifestation
To that Rāmakṛṣṇa, embodiment of Divine sport, ever blissful — my salutation.

*10*

सर्वधर्मप्रणेतारं धर्मग्लानिविनाशकम् ।
साधुमित्रं शिवं शान्तं रामकृष्णं नमाम्यहम् ।

*Sarva-dharma-praṇetāraṁ dharma-glāni-vināśakam* |
*sādhu-mitraṁ śivaṁ śāntaṁ Rāmakṛṣṇaṁ namāmy aham* ||

The proclaimer of all Dharmas, the burnisher of fading virtue,
The friend of the pious, and a centre of divine bliss and peace,
To Him Rāmakṛṣṇa, my salutation.

*11*

अज्ञानतिमिरे यस्तु ज्ञानालोकप्रदीपकः ।
विमलानन्ददानाय प्रादुरासीन् महीतले ।
नमोऽस्तु रामकृष्णाय तस्मै श्री गुरवे नमः ॥

*Ajñāna-timire yas tu jñān'ā-loka-pradīpakaḥ* |
*vimalānanda-dānāya prādurāsīn mahītale* |
*namo'stu Rāmakṛṣṇāya tasmai śrī-gurave namaḥ* ||

Lighting the luminous lamp of wisdom, He stands as the dispeller of the darkness of ignorance.
He has come again to this world of ours to bestow the highest bliss on all —
To Him Rāmakṛṣṇa the World-Teacher, my salutations.

*12*

संसारार्णवघोरे यः कर्णधारस्वरूपकः ।
नमोऽस्तु रामकृष्णाय तस्मै श्री गुरवे नमः ॥

*Samsār'ārṇva-ghore yaḥ karṇa-dhāra-svarūpakaḥ* |
*namo'stu Rāmakṛṣṇāya tasmai śrī-gurave namaḥ* ||

He who is like the captain of a ferry-boat to those sinking in the terrible ocean of Samsāra,
To Him Rāmakṛṣṇa the World-Teacher, my salutations.

*13*

त्वं हि विष्णुर्विरिञ्चिस्त्वं त्वञ्च देवो महेश्वरः
त्वञ्चैव शक्तिरूपोऽसि निर्गुणस्त्वं सनातनः ।
त्वां स्तोतुं कोऽत्र शक्तः स्याद्भावातीतमनामयम्
भगवन् सर्वभूतात्मन् रामकृष्ण नमोऽस्तु ते ॥

*Tvam hi Viṣṇur Viriñcis tvaṁ tvam ca devo-Maheś varaḥ* |
*tvaṁ ca'iva Śakti-rupo'si nirguṇas tvaṁ sanātanaḥ* |
*tvāṁ stotum ko'tra śaktaḥ syād bhāvātītam anāmayam* |
*bhagavan sarva-bhūtātman Rāmakṛṣṇa namo'stu te* ||

Thou art Viṣṇu and Thou art Brahmā,
Thou art also the great Lord Maheśvara;
Thou art Śakti, the great Mother of the Universe;
And Thou art also the Transcendent Being unconnected with the Guṇas of Prakṛti.
O Lord of abounding glory, Thou the indweller in all!
No praise can exhaust even a part of the greatness of Thine, who art beyond the purview of thought and free from decay.
To Thee Rāmakṛṣṇa the soul of all, my salutations!

*14*

सर्वाय सर्वपाराय सर्वभावस्वरूपिणे
सर्वभावविहीनाय रामकृष्णाय ते नमः ॥

*Sarvāya sarva-pārāya sarva-bhāva-svarūpiṇe |*
*sarva-bhāva-vihīnāya Rāmakṛṣṇāya te namaḥ||*

O Thou, the all-encompassing yet also the Transcendent!
O Thou, the embodiment of all spiritual sentiments but also the Pure Consciousness beyond all sentiments!
To Thee Rāmakṛṣṇa, my salutations!

*15*

महामायास्वरूपाय महामोहविनाशिने ।
मायातीताय शान्ताय रामकृष्णाय ते नमः ॥

*Mahā-māyā-svarūpāya mahā-moha-vināśine |*
*māyā tītāya śāntāya Rāmakṛṣṇāya te namaḥ ||*

Thou art the embodiment of Mahāmāya and the eradicator of basic ignorance!
To Thee Rāmakṛṣṇa, who transcends Māyā and art established in Peace, my salutations!

*16*

निरञ्जनं नित्यमनन्तरूपं भक्तानुकम्पाधृतविग्रहं वै ।
ईशावतारं परमेशमीड्यं तं रामकृष्णं शिरसा नमामि ॥

*Nirañjanaṁ nityam ananta-rūpam*
*bhaktā'nukampā-dhṛta-vigrahaṁ vai |*
*īśāvatāraṁ parameśam īḍyam*
*taṁ Rāmakṛṣṇaṁ śirasā namāmi ||*

Thou the stainless, eternal and multiformed one,
Who hast assumed a form out of Thy abounding grace to devotees;
Thou, the worshipful Lord of all, manifest as the Divine Incarnate,
To Thee Ramakṛṣṇa, my full prostration with head touching the ground.

# ŚRĪ RĀMAKṚṢṆĀVATĀRA STOTRAM
## By Swāmī Abhedānanda

*1*

हृदयकमलमध्ये राजितं निर्विकल्पं
सदसदखिलभेदातीतमेकस्वरूपम् ।
प्रकृतिविकृतिशून्यं नित्यमानन्दमूर्तिं
विमलपरमहंसं रामकृष्णं भजामः ॥

*Hṛdaya-kamala-madhye rājitaṁ nirvikalpaṁ*
*sad-asad-akhila-bhed'ātītam eka-svarūpam* |
*prakṛti vikṛti-śūnyaṁ nityam ānanda-mūrtim*
*vimala-paramahaṁsaṁ Rāmakṛṣṇaṁ bhajāmaḥ* ||

The changeless Absolute shining bright in the lotus of the heart,
The Unitary Being beyond the grasp of concepts like existence and non-existence,
And devoid of the modifications of Nature — thus abides the blissful being of Rāmakṛṣṇa.
To Him the spotless Spiritual Swan, our salutation.

*2*

निरूपममतिसूक्ष्मं निष्प्रपञ्चं निरीहं
गगनसदृशमीशं सर्वभूताधिवासम् ।

त्रिगुणरहितसच्चिद्ब्रह्मरूपं वरेण्यम्
विमलपरमहंसं रामकृष्णं भजामः ॥

*Nirupamam ati sūkṣmaṁ niṣprapañcaṁ nirīham*
*gagana-sadṛśam īśaṁ sarva-bhūt'ādhi-vāsam* |
*triguṇa-rahita-saccid-brahma-rūpaṁ vareṇyam*
*vimala-paramahaṁsaṁ Rāmakṛṣṇaṁ bhajāmaḥ* ||

Imcomparable, subtlest of the subtle, acosmic and desireless,
The Supreme Being resembling the sky in all-pervasiveness,
And providing in Himself the home for all beings to rest,
The most Worshipful Being, Brahman, the Existence – Knowledge – Bliss Absolute, beyond the pale of the three Guṇas of Prakṛti —
To Thee, Rāmakṛṣṇa, the spotless Spiritual Swan, our salutation.

*3*

प्रलयजलधिमग्नं वेदराशिं दिधीर्षु-
र्दनुजमतिविशालं हंसि शंखं विचित्रम् ।
तमपरिमितवीर्यं मीनरूपं दधानं
विमलपरमहंसं रामकृष्णं भजामः ॥

*Pralaya-jaladhi-magnaṁ vedarāśiṁ didhīrṣur–*
*danujam ati-viśālaṁ haṁsi śaṅkhaṁ vicitram* |
*tam aparimita-vīryaṁ mīnarūpaṁ dadhānaṁ*
*vimala-paramahaṁsaṁ Rāmakṛṣṇaṁ bhajāmaḥ* ||

Resolved to salvage the Vedas from the waters of the Deluge,
Thou didst destroy Śaṅkha, a huge and astounding Asura who had hidden the Vedas in the Pralaya waters,
Assuming the form of a Fish, peerless in strength —
To Him Rāmakṛṣṇa, the spotless Spiritual Swan, our salutation.

*4*

अतुल-विपुलदेहे चिन्मये कूर्मरूपे
वहसि सकलमेतद्विश्वमाधारशक्त्या ।
तव खलु महिमानं कोऽल्पधीर्वर्णयेत् त्वां
विमलपरमहंसं रामकृष्णं भजामः ॥

*Atula-vipula-dehe cinmaye kūrma-rūpe*
*vahasi sakalam etad viśvam ādhāra-śaktyā* |
*tava khalu mahimāṇam ko'lpadhīr varṇayet tvām*
*vimala-paramahaṁsaṁ Rāmakṛṣṇaṁ bhajāmaḥ* ||

In Thy Incarnation as the Cosmic-Tortoise, assuming a body incomparable in size and constituted of pure Consciousness-Bliss
Thou, the world's supporting power, didst bear on Thy back the entire cosmos.
How can I, a creature of little intelligence, describe this great act of Thine?
To Him Rāmakṛṣṇa, the spotless Spiritual Swan, our salutation.

*5*

दशन-विधृत-पृथ्वीं शूकरं श्वेतकायं
दलित-दितिजराजं दंष्ट्रिणं चक्रपाणिम् ।
अमितविभवशक्तिं पालकं देवतानां
विमलपरमहंसं रामकृष्णं भजामः ॥

*Daśana-vidhṛta-pṛthvīṁ śūkaraṁ śvetakāyaṁ*
*dalita-ditijarājaṁ daṁṣṭriṇaṁ cakra-pāṇim* |
*amita-vibhava-śaktiṁ pālakaṁ devatānām*
*vimala-paramahaṁsaṁ Rāmakṛṣṇaṁ bhajāmaḥ* ||

Assuming the form of a White Boar, Thou, the discus-armed and the fierce-fanged of immeasurable might,
Didst support the earth on Thy fangs, slaying Hiraṇyākṣa, and offer protection to the Devas.
To Him Rāmakṛṣṇa, the spotless Spiritual Swan, our salutation.!

*6*

विकट-दशनवक्त्रं लोलजिह्वं प्रचण्डं
गिरिवर-समकायं रक्तहस्तं नृसिंहम् ।
प्रशमित-सुरखेदं कोटिसूर्यप्रकाशं
विमलपरमहंसं रामकृष्णं भजामः ॥

*Vikaṭa-daśana-vaktraṁ lola-jihvaṁ pracaṇḍam*
*girivara-sama-kāyaṁ rakta-hastaṁ nṛsiṁham* |
*praśamita-sura-khedaṁ kotisūrya-prakāśam*
*vimala-paramahaṁsaṁ Rāmakṛṣṇaṁ bhajāmaḥ* ||

With a face set with terrific teeth and with tongue
lolling from the mouth,
A body of mountainous proportion, and red-palmed—
Thus shaped as a Man-Lion with the lustre of countless
suns,
Thou didst give relief to the sufferings of Devas and
holy men.
To Him Rāmakṛṣṇa, the spotless Spiritual Swan, our
salutation!

7

छलयितुमवतीर्णो वामनस्त्वं बलिं वै
त्रिचरणकमलेन क्रामसि स्वर्भुवो भूः ।
परमपुरुषमादिं काश्यपं विश्वरूपं
विमलपरमहंसं रामकृष्णं भजामः ॥

*Chalayitum avatīrṇo Vāmanas tvaṁ Baliṁ vai*
*tri-caraṇa-kamalena krāmasi svar-bhuvo-bhūḥ* |
*parama-puruṣam ādiṁ Kāśyapaṁ viśvarūpam*
*vimala-paramahaṁsaṁ Rāmakṛṣṇaṁ bhajāmaḥ* ||

Thou, the Supreme Being and the All-formed, born as
Vāmana the Dwarf, as Kasyapa's son,
By a strategem didst measure and take possession of
the three worlds, Bhū, Bhuvaḥ and Svaḥ, from Bali
by three strides —
To Him Rāmakṛṣṇa, the spotless Spiritual Swan, our
salutation!

*8*

निशित-परशुधारं क्षत्रसन्तानकेतुं
नवजलधरवर्णं भार्गवं भीमवीर्यम् ।
शमनसदृश घोरं जामदग्न्यं विशाल
विमलपरमहंसं रामकष्णं भजामः ॥

*Niśita-paraśudhāraṁ kṣatra-santāna-ketum*
*nava-jaladhara-varṇaṁ bhārgavaṁ bhīma-vīryam* |
*śamana-sadṛśa-ghoram jāmadagnyam viśālam*
*vimala-paramahaṁsaṁ Rāmakṛṣṇaṁ bhajāmaḥ* ||

Thou didst incarnate in the line of Bhṛgu as Rāma, Jamadagni's son,
Armed with a sharp battle axe, and resembling a fresh rain cloud in complexion,
Mighty in puissance and fierce like Yama himself, whose advent marked the doom of Kṣatriya clans —
To Him Rāmakṛṣṇa, the spotless Spiritual Swan, our salutation!

*9*

रघुकुलवरमीशं जानकीप्राणनाथं
समरकुशलवीरं राघवं रावणारिम् ।
हनुमदनुजसेव्यं धार्मिकं सत्यपालं
विमलपरमहंसं रामकृष्णं भजामः ॥

*Raghu-kula-varam īśaṁ jānakī-prāṇanātham*
*samara-kuśala-vīraṁ Rāghavaṁ Rāvaṇārim* |
*Hanumad-anuja-sevyam dhārmikaṁ satyapālam*
*vimala-paramahaṁsaṁ Rāmakṛṣṇaṁ bhajāmaḥ* ||

Born as the noblest prince in the house of Raghu, Thou wert Rāma, the dear consort of Sītā and foe of Rāvaṇa;
Warlike and devoted to truth, Thou wert the protector of Dharma, ever served by Hanumān and Thy brothers.
To Him Rāmakṛṣṇa, the spotless Spiritual Swan, our salutation!

*10*

हलधरमतिशुभ्रं नीलवस्त्रं सुरेन्द्रं
दनुज-दलनकार्ये पारगं मत्तसिंहम् ।
यममिव यमुनाया भीतिदं रौहिणेयं
विमलपरमहंसं रामकृष्णं भजामः ॥

*Hala-dharam-ati-śubhraṁ nīla-vastraṁ surendram*
*danuja-dalana-kārye pāragaṁ matta-simham* |
*yamam iva yamunāyā bhītidaṁ rauhiṇeyam*
*vimala-paramahaṁsaṁ Rāmakṛṣṇaṁ bhajāmaḥ* ||

Thou wert Balarāma the son of Rohiṇī, very fair in complexion and wearing a blue apparel and armed with a plough-weapon;
Like a furious lion, Thou wert ever prompt in decimating the tribe of Rākṣasas,
And like Yama Himself, Thou didst frighten the Yamunā.
To Him Rāmakṛṣṇa, the spotless Spiritual Swan, our salutation!

*11*

व्रजविपिनविहारे श्यामलं वासुदेवं
सुमधुररसकेलिं गोपिकाप्राणनाथम् ।
मदनरमणवेषं कंसकालं कवीशं
विमलपरमहंसं रामकृष्णं भजामः ॥

*Vraja-vipina-vihāre śyāmalaṁ Vāsudevam*
*sumadhura-rasa-keliṁ gopikā-prāṇanātham* |
*madana-ramaṇa-veṣaṁ Kaṁsakālaṁ kavīśaṁ*
*vimala-paramahaṁsaṁ Rāmakṛṣṇaṁ bhajāmaḥ* ||

Born as Vasudeva's black-hued son Kṛṣṇa, the killer of Kaṁsa and possessed of beauty and wisdom unrivalled,
Thou wert noted for Thy sports in the woodlands of Vraja —
Sports in which Thou, the beloved of the Gopikās,
Didst exemplify the sweetness of Madhura Bhāva —
To Him Rāmakṛṣṇa, the spotless Spiritual Swan, our salutations!

*12*

पशुवधमतिघोरं चोदितं वेदशास्त्रैः
शमयितुमवतीर्णं ज्ञानदं शाक्यसिंहम् ।
प्रकटितनवमार्गं श्लिष्टनिर्वाणकल्पं
विमलपरमहंसं रामकृष्णं भजामः ॥

*Paśuvadham atighoraṁ coditaṁ veda-śāstraiḥ*
*śamayitum avatīrṇaṁ jñānadaṁ śākyasiṁham* |

*prakaṭita navamārg'ādvaita-nirvvāṇa-kalpam*
*vimala-paramahaṁsaṁ Rāmakṛṣṇaṁ bhajāmaḥ* ||

Thou wert embodied as the Buddha, the lion of the Śākya clan and the bestower of spiritual illumination,
Whose mission it was to stop the cruel slaughter of animals justified as a Vedic commandment,
And lay down the novel path of non-duality known also as Nirvāṇa.
To Him Rāmakṛṣṇa, the spotless Spiritual Swan, our salutation!

*13*

मधुरसरलवाक्यैरीशतत्त्वं प्रकाश्य
क्रुशगतपरिशेषोऽपीशपुत्रोऽमृतो यः ।
तमतिशयपवित्रं मेरिजं लोकबन्धुं
विमलपरमहंसं रामकृष्णं भजामः ॥

*Madhura-sarala-vākyair īśatattvam prakāśya*
*kruśa-gata-pariśeṣo'pīśa-putro'mṛto yaḥ*
*tam atiśaya-pavitraṁ Merijaṁ loka-bandhum*
*vimala-paramahaṁsaṁ Rāmakṛṣṇaṁ bhajāmaḥ* ||

Born of Mary as saviour of the world, Thou, the embodiment of purity, preached the truth of God in a sweet and simple way,
And though crucified, proved immortal, being the Son of God—
To Thee Rāmakṛṣṇa, the spotless Spiritual Swan, our salutation!

*14*

श्रुतिनिगदितमार्गस्थापनायावतारं
जिननयबहुवादभ्रान्तिमुन्मूलयन्तम् ।
भुवनविजयकीर्तिं शङ्करं भाष्यकारं
विमलपरमहंसं रामकृष्णं भजामः ॥

*Śruti-nigadita-mārga-sthāpanāy'āvatāram*
*jina-naya-bahuvāda-bhrāntim unmūlayantam* |
*bhuvana-vijaya-kīrtiṁ śaṅkaraṁ bhāṣyakāram*
*vimala paramahaṁsaṁ Rāmakṛṣṇaṁ bhajāmaḥ* ||

To establish the way of spiritual life laid down in the Veda,
Refuting the many specious arguments raised against it by hostile atheistic thinkers,
Thou wert born as Śaṅkara, the scriptural commentator of world-wide fame —
To Him Rāmakṛṣṇa, the spotless Spiritual Swan, our salutation.

*15*

कलिमलहरनाम्नः कीर्तयन् घोषयन्तं
करधृतजलपात्रं दण्डिनं हेमवर्णम् ।
भवजलनिधिपोतं कृष्णचैतन्यरूपं
विमलपरमहंसं रामकृष्णं भजामः ॥

*Kali-mala-hara-nāmnaḥ kīrtayan ghoṣayantam*
*kara-dhṛta-jala-pātraṁ daṇḍinaṁ hema-varṇam* |

*bhava-jala-nidhi-potaṁ Kṛṣṇa-caitanya-rūpam*
*vimala-paramahaṁsaṁ Rāmakṛṣṇaṁ bhajāmaḥ* ||

Singing aloud the Lord's name that destroys the evil of Kali,
And carrying a water pot and a staff in hand,
Thou didst incarnate as Kṛṣṇa-Caitanya of golden hue,
A veritable ferry boat to those seeking to cross the ocean of Saṁsāra —
To Him Rāmakṛṣṇa, the spotless Spiritual Swan, our salutation!

*16*

वितरितुमवतीर्णं ज्ञानभक्तिप्रशान्तीः
प्रणयगलितचित्तं जीवदुःखासहिष्णुम् ।
धृतसहजसमाधिं चिन्मयं कोमलाङ्गं
विमलपरमहंसं रामकृष्णं भजामः ॥

*Vitaritum avatīrṇaṁ jñāna-bhakti-praśāntīḥ*
*praṇaya-galita-cittaṁ jīva-duḥkh'āsahiṣṇum* |
*dhṛta-sahaja-samādhiṁ cinmayaṁ komalāṅgaṁ*
*vimala-paramahaṁsaṁ Rāmakṛṣṇaṁ bhajāmaḥ* ||

With a heart bending with universal love that could never bear to see the misery of Jīvas,
Thou art now born as Rāmakṛṣṇa to bestow Knowledge, Devotion and Peace on mankind.
Thou whose hallowed form was of the pure Radiance of Intelligence,

And whose mind, poised on the threshold of relative consciousness, was habitually in the Transcendent State —
To Him Rāmakṛṣṇa, the spotless Spiritual Swan, our salutation!

*17*

हरिहरविधिदेवा मूर्तिभेदास्तवैते
निरुपमबहुमूर्तिर्मायया कल्पयन्तम्
अमितगुणचरित्रं दीनबन्धुं दयालुं
विमलपरमहंसं रामकृष्णं भजामः ॥

*Hari-Hara-Vidhi-devā mūrti-bhedās tav'aite*
*nirupama-bahu mūrtir māyayā kalpayantam* |
*Amita-guṇa-caritraṁ dīnabandhum dayālum*
*vimala-paramahaṁsaṁ Rāmakṛṣṇaṁ bhajāmaḥ* ||

Hari, Hara and Vidhi are but the three aspects of Thy being;
And by the power of Thy Māyā, countless and wondrous are the forms Thou manifestest.
Friend of the afflicted and compassion's embodiment!
No bounds there are for thy excellences —
To Him Rāmakṛṣṇa, the spotless Spiritual Swan, our salutation!

*18*

जय जय करुणाब्धे मोक्षसेतो स्मरारे
जय जय जगदीश ज्ञानसिन्धो स्वयम्भो ।

जय जय परमात्मंस्त्राहि मां भक्तिहीनं
जय जय भवहारिन् रामकृष्ण द्विबाहो ॥

*Jayajaya karuṇābdhe mokṣa-seto smarāre*
*jaya jaya jagadīśa jñāna-sindho svayambho* |
*jaya jaya param'ātmaṁs trāhi māṁ bhakti-hīnam*
*jaya jaya bhava-hārin Rāmakṛṣṇa dvi bāho* ||

Hail to Thee, the destroyer of lust, the ocean of mercy and the bridge to liberation's shore!
Hail to Thee, the self-born Lord of the universe, and sea of wisdom!
Hail to Thee, the Supreme! Thou the Saviour even of devotionless one like me!
Hail to Thee, Rāmakṛṣṇa, the two-armed destroyer of worldliness!

*19*

मूकोऽहं नाभिजानामि तव स्तोत्र जगद्गुरो ।
तथापि त्वत्कृपालेशाद्वाचालोऽस्मि पुनः पुनः ॥

*Mūko'haṁ nābhijānāmi tava stotram jagadguro* |
*tathāpi tvad kṛpā-leśād vācālo'smi punaḥ punaḥ* ||

I am as good as a dumb creature, O World-Teacher! and I do not know how to glorify Thee.
Yet by a particle of Thy grace I am stimulated to eloquence again and again!

## BHAJA RĀMAKṚṢṆA STOTRAM
### By Swāmī Abhedānanda

*1*

रे भ्रान्त भोगविषयेषु कथं हि रक्तो
मोहं गतो भ्रमसि वर्त्मनि दीर्घकालम् ।
विश्रान्तिमिच्छसि यदि ह्यनिशं सुखाब्धौ
सन्तापसंसृतिहरं भज रामकृष्णम् ॥

*Re bhrānta bhoga-viṣayeṣu katham hi rakto*
*mohaṁ gato bhramasi vartmani dīrgha-kālam|*
*viśrāntim icchasi yadi hy'aniśaṁ sukhābdhau*
*santāpa-saṁsṛti-haraṁ bhaja Rāmakṛṣṇam ||*

O witless one! Long hast thou been wandering about along the paths of Saṁsāra, a deluded wayfarer,
Drawn by thy attachments for the objects of the senses.
If rest in the Eternal Sea of Peace is what thou seekest,
Then seek refuge in Rāmakṛṣṇa, the destroyer of man's woes of transmigratory existence.

*2*

दुर्वारघोर-भवदाव-विदह्यमानो
जङ्गम्यसे मलिनवासनया सुखाप्त्यै ।

नीचाश्रयं कथमहो यदि शान्तिकामः
संतापसंसृतिहरं भज रामकृष्णम् ॥

*Durvāra-ghora-bhava-dāva-vidahyamāno*
*jaṅgamyase malina-vāsanayā sukh'āptyai* |
*nīcāśrayam katham aho yadi śānti-kāmaḥ*
*santāpa-saṁsṛti-haraṁ bhaja Rāmakṛṣṇam* ||

Driven by Thy own evil tendencies to seek pleasure,
Thou art, O man, being burnt in the terrible forest fire of Saṁsāra.
If thou art seeking for peace, why resort to ignoble supports?
Come and seek refuge in Rāmakṛṣṇa, the destroyer of man's woes of transmigratory existence.

3

शास्त्रेष्वनात्मसु कथं हि तव प्रवृत्तिः
दुस्तर्कजालमिह देशिकवाग्विरुद्धम् ।
सिद्धान्तहीनमपि सन्त्यज मन्दबुध्दे
सन्देहविभ्रमहरं भज रामकृष्णम् ॥

*Śāstreṣv'anātmasu katham hi tava pravṛttiḥ*
*dustarka-jālam iha deśika-vāg-viruddham* |
*siddhānta-hīnam api santyaja manda-buddhe*
*sandeha vibhrama haraṁ bhaja Rāmakṛṣṇam* ||

Why this engrossment on thy part with doctrines that are purely atheistic in import?
They are full of perverse arguments that go against the Guru's instruction.
Seeing that they convey no firm conclusion on life's mystery, abandon them, O thou of poor understanding,
And adore Rāmakṛṣṇa, the destroyer of all confusion caused by doubts.

*4*

स्त्रीकाञ्चनादिषु सदा यदि तेऽनुरक्ति -
स्तृष्णाक्षयो न भविता कथमप्यमीषु ।
विज्ञाय तान्निगडवद् भवबन्धहेतून्
सन्त्यक्तकामकनकं भज रामकृष्णम् ॥

*Strī-kāñcanādiṣu sadā yadi te'nuraktis -*
*tṛṣṇākṣayo na bhavitā katham apy'amīṣu* |
*vijñāya tān nigaḍavad bhava-bandha-hetūn*
*santyakta kāma-kanakam bhaja Rāmakṛṣṇam* ||

If thy longing is for indulgence in sexual pleasures and pursuit of wealth,
Know that the thirst for them shall never be quenched, however much thou might enjoy.
Knowing them as fetters binding thee to the transmigratory cycle, reject them,
And worship Rāmakṛṣṇa, the renouncer of lust and gold.

*5*

भार्यामशेषगुण-भूषित-भक्ति-युक्तां
योषाञ्च कामवशगां सकलां तथैव ।
दूरात् प्रणम्य जितवान् य उ मातृबुद्ध्या
तं कामगन्धरहितं भज रामकृष्णम् ॥

*Bhāryām aśeṣa-guṇa-bhūṣita-bhakti-yuktāṁ*
*yoṣāñ ca kāma-vaśagāṁ sakalām tath'aiva* |
*dūrāt praṇamya jitavān ya u mātṛ-buddhyā*
*taṁ kāma-gandha-rahitaṁ bhaja Rāmakṛṣṇam* ||

Seeing them both — his wedded wife, devoted and virtuous, on the one hand,
And a woman, lusty and love-lorn, on the other —
Alike as manifestations of Divine Motherhood,
He saluted them from afar and came out victorious.
Him Rāmakṛṣṇa, devoid of the slightest taint of lust, do thou adore.

*6*

संस्पृश्य धातुनिचयान् परिकम्पिताङ्गः
संज्ञाविहीन इव यो विकृताङ्गुलिश्च ।
सद्योऽभवज्जडवदिन्द्रियवृत्तिशून्य-
स्तं त्यागपारगमहो भज रामकृष्णम् ॥

*Saṁspṛśya dhātu nicayān pari-kaṁpit'āṅgaḥ*
*saṁjñā-vihīna iva yo vikṛt'āṅguliś ca* |
*sadyo'bhavaj jaḍavad indriya-vṛtti-śūnyas —*
*tam tyāga - pāragam aho bhaja Rāmakṛṣṇam* ||

At the touch of any metal he felt shocked,
And his fingers contorted as of one that had fallen into a fit.
And his sense organs all stopped functioning as of an inert person.
Him, Rāmakṛṣṇa, the very embodiment of renunciation, do thou adore.

7

प्रेम्नः स्वरूपमिह यद्विमलं पवित्रं
निःस्वार्थमित्यभिधया कथितं सुबोधैः ।
तत् प्राप्तुमिच्छसि यदि प्रणयार्द्रचित्तान्
कुर्वन्तमाश्रितजनान् भज रामकृष्णम् ॥

*Premnaḥ svarūpam iha yad vimalam pavitraṁ*
*niḥ-svārtham ity'abhidhayā kathitaṁ subodhaiḥ* |
*tat prāptum icchasi yadi praṇay'ārdra-cittān*
*kurvantam āśrita-janān bhaja Rāmakṛṣṇam* ||

If thou aspirest for the state of selflessness,
Called as the holy, pure and motiveless love by enlightened men,
Then do thou adore Rāmakṛṣṇa, who saturates the hearts of his devotees with love.

8

स्नेहो हि मातुरिह कारण-सन्निबद्धो
भ्रातुस्तथा पितुरयं नं च हेतुशून्यः ।
यत् प्रेम हेतुरहितं न हि केन तुल्यं
तं प्रेमसिन्धुसदृशं भज रामकृष्णम् ॥

*Sneho hi mātur iha kāraṇa - sannibaddho*
*bhrātus tathā pitur ayam na ca hetu-śūnyaḥ* |
*yat prema hetu-rahitaṁ na hi kena tulyaṁ*
*taṁ prema-sindhu-sadṛśaṁ bhaja Rāmakṛṣṇam* ||

The love of a mother has a motive behind it.
So too the love of a brother or a father is not without a motive.
But unmotivated and without anything equal to it is the love of Rāmakṛṣṇa —
Him do thou adore, who was verily like an ocean of love.

*9*

प्राप्ते यथा प्रियतमे ललना प्रसन्ना
दूरं गते भवति भाव-विकार-युक्ता ।
आराद्गते प्रियतमे च तथा स्वभक्ते
प्रेष्ठायमानमिह तं भज रामकृष्णम् ॥

*Prāpte yathā priyatame lalanā prasannā*
*dūram gate bhavati bhāva-vikāra-yuktā* |
*ārād-gate priyatame ca tathā svabhakte*
*preṣṭhāyamānam iha tam bhaja Rāmakṛṣṇam* ||

A woman is all joy when her beloved has come.
When he is away, her mind is filled with anxious thoughts.
Likewise he was, his mind overflowing with love when his disciples approached him,
Him Rāmakṛṣṇa do thou adore!

*10*

येनाति-दुःखविकृता भजनानुरागः ।
शुद्धीकृताः प्रियकथा-करुणा-कटाक्षैः ।
आश्वासिताः प्रतिदिनं पुरुषार्थकामा -
स्तं धर्ममोक्षदमहो भज रामकृष्णम् ॥

*Yen'āti duḥkha-vikṛtā bhajan'ānurāgaḥ*
*śuddhīkṛtāḥ priyakathā-karuṇā-kaṭākṣaiḥ* |
*āśvāsitāḥ prati-dinam puruṣārtha-kāmās-*
*tam dharma-mokṣadam aho bhaja Rāmakṛṣṇam* ||

He whose loving speech and gracious look purified and consoled spiritual aspirants
Stricken with the anguish of longing and seeking life's fulfilment —
Him, Rāmakṛṣṇa, the grantor of moral excellence and liberation, do thou adore.

*11*

योगैश्च साधनशतैः फलमाप्यते यत्
यद्वा सुखं भवति चित्तनिरोधनेन ।
यत् सन्निधिं मुहुरुपेत्य पुमान् भजेत्तत्
तं शान्तिशर्मदमहो भज रामकृष्णम् ॥

*Yogaiś ca sādhana-śataiḥ phalam āpyate yat*
*yad vā sukham bhavati citta-nirodhanena* |
*yat sannidhiṁ muhur upetya pumān bhajet tat*
*taṁ śānti-śarmadam aho bhaja Rāmakṛṣṇam* ||

The fruits that Yoga and other practices confer on one,
The bliss that accrues to one who has established control over the senses —
He whose very proximity conferred these blessings on man,
Him Rāmakṛṣṇa, the bestower of Peace, do thou adore.

*12*

नारायणं हि पुरुषं पुरुषं प्रतीतं
दृष्ट्वा शिवाञ्च रमणीं रमणीं प्रतीताम् ।
भृत्यायतेऽप्यखिल भूतमहेश्वरो य-
स्तं स्वाभिमानरहितं भज रामकृष्णम् ॥

*Nārāyaṇaṁ hi puruṣaṁ puruṣaṁ pratītam*
*dṛṣṭvā śivāñ ca ramaṇīṁ ramaṇīṁ pratītām* |
*bhṛtyāyate'pyakhila-bhūta-maheśvaro yas-*
*taṁ svābhimāna-rahitaṁ bhaja Rāmakṛṣṇam* ||

Whichever man he saw, He saw Him as Nārāyaṇa,
And whichever woman he saw, He saw her as the Mother Divine.
Though the Lord of all, He behaved as the servant of all —
Adore Him, Rāmakṛṣṇa, who was without a trace of self-conscious pride.

*13*

नाधीतशास्त्र इह योऽखिलशास्त्रवेत्ता
नाधीतवेद इह यः श्रुतिसारविज्ञः ।

नाधीततन्त्र इह यः कुलधर्मवक्ता
तं तत्त्वबोधकमहो भज रामकृष्णम् ॥

*N'ādhīta-śāstra iha yo'khila-śāstra-vettā*
*n'ādhīta-veda iha yaḥ śruti-sāra-vijñaḥ* |
*n'ādhīta-tantra iha yaḥ kula-dharma-vaktā*
*taṁ tattva-bhodhakam aho bhaja Rāmakṛṣṇam* ||

Though not a student of the Śāstras, He knew all the Śāstras;
Though not a student of the Vedas, He knew the essence of all Vedas;
And though not a student of the Tantras, he was an adept in the ways of the Mother cult.
Worship Him, Rāmakṛṣṇa, the transmitter of the knowledge of Truth Supreme.

*14*

निर्वासनोऽपि सततं परमङ्गलार्थी
निष्कर्मकोऽपि सततं परकर्मकर्ता
निर्दुःखलेशमपि तं सततं परेषां
दुःखेषु कातरमहो भज रामकृष्णम् ॥

*Nirvāsano'pi satataṁ para-maṅgal'ārthī*
*niṣkarmako'pi satataṁ para-karma kartā* |
*nirduḥkha-leśam api taṁ satataṁ pareṣām*
*duḥkheṣu kātaram aho bhaja Rāmakṛṣṇam* ||

His mind was free from every form of desire, gross or subtle, yet he prayed for the welfare of others.
He was free from the bondage of all action,
Yet He worked for the welfare of others.
Though Himself free from every form of sorrow and suffering,
He felt the utmost distress in the sufferings of others.
Adore Him Rāmakṛṣṇa, who thus felt the sorrows of others as his.

*15*

भक्तैः सदा परिवृतो निजपार्षदैर्यो
गायन् हसन् भगवतः सुखयन् प्रसङ्गैः ।
तारागणैरिव विधुर्द्युतिमत्र धत्ते
तं स्वर्गशर्मदमहो भज रामकृष्णम् ॥

*Bhaktaiḥ sadā parivṛto nija-pārṣadair yo*
*gāyan hasan bhagavataḥ sukhayan prasaṅgaiḥ* |
*tārāgaṇair iva vidhur dyutim atra dhatte*
*taṁ svarga-śarmadam aho bhaja Rāmakṛṣṇam* ||

Surrounded always by devotees, His constant attendants,
And ever singing, laughing, and talking about the Lord in their midst,
He shone like the moon attended by the stars,
Worship Him Rāmakṛṣṇa who was thus the bestower of the bliss of heaven to all who went to Him.

*16*

शाक्तैः शिवेति शिव इत्यपि शंभुभक्तैः
कृष्णावतार इति वैष्णवशेखरैश्च ।

ज्ञानीति यः परमहंस इतीह धीरैः
संज्ञायते च तमहो भज रामकृष्णम् ॥

*Śāktaiḥ Śive'ti Śiva ity'api śambhu-bhaktaiḥ*
*Kṛṣṇ'āvatāra iti vaiṣṇava-śekharaiś ca*
*jñānī'ti yaḥ paramahaṁsa itīha dhīraiḥ*
*saṁjñāyate ca tam aho bhaja Rāmakṛṣṇam* ||

The Śāktas called Him the Mother and the Śaivites, Śiva;
The best among Vaiṣṇavas looked upon Him as the incarnation of Kṛṣṇa;
And the wise ones called Him the all-knowing Paramahaṁsa.
Worship Him Rāmakṛṣṇa in whom all found the fulfilment of their ideals.

*17*

भ्रमन् नानायोनौ बहुविधशरीरं परिगतः
सुखं नाल्पं लेभे कनक-युवती-भोग विषयैः ।
इदानीं ज्ञात्वा त्वां प्रणतसुहृदं शान्तिसुखदं
विरक्तोऽहं याचे तव चरणयोर्भक्तिमचलाम् ॥

*Bhraman nānā-yonau bahuvidha - śarīraṁ parigataḥ*
*sukhaṁ n'ālpaṁ lebhe kanaka-yuvatī-bhoga-viṣayaiḥ* |
*idānīṁ jñātvā tvāṁ praṇata-suhṛdaṁ śānti-sukhadam*
*virakto'haṁ yāce tava caraṇayor bhaktim acalām* ||

Transmigrating from body to body and pursuing pleasure and wealth,
I know not what real happiness is.
Knowing of Thee now — Thou the friend of the refugees and bestower of peace —
I seek pure devotion for Thy feet, having abandoned all attachment for the objects of sensate life.

*18*

गृहीत्वा भ्रान्तं मां कुमतिविषयाशापरिवृतं
सदा रक्ष ब्रह्मन् कुपथगमनात्‌दुःखगहनात् ।
कृपासारान् प्राणे वितर सततं शोकदलिते
विवेकं वैराग्यं परममपि मे देहि भगवन् ।।

*Gṛhītvā bhrāntaṁ māṁ kumati-viṣayāśā-parivṛtaṁ*
*sadā rakṣa brahman kupatha-gamanād duḥkha-gahanāt* |
*kṛpāsārān prāṇe vitara satataṁ śokadalite*
*vivekaṁ vairāgyaṁ paramam api me dehi bhagavan* ||

Holding me by the hand, draw me away, O Lord Supreme, from the path of evil —
From amidst the objects of sense life and the depth of grief;
Sprinkle for ever more the water of Thy grace on my mind tortured by sorrows;
And bestow on me discrimination and renunciation of the highest order.

*19*

यो भजेत् परया भक्त्या रामकृष्णं भवान्तकम् ।
भवबन्धात् स निर्मुक्तो भवेत् सद्यो न संशयः ॥

*Yo bhajet parayā bhaktyā Rāmakṛṣṇam bhavāntakam* |
*bhava-bandhāt sa nirmukto bhavet sadyo na saṁśayaḥ* ||

Whoever adores with supreme devotion Rāmakṛṣṇa, the effacer of entanglement in transmigratory existence,
He is sure to be released soon from the bondage of worldly life — there is no doubt about it.

# ŚRĪ RĀMAKṚṢṆA-STAVARĀJAḤ
## By Swāmī Abhedānanda

*1*

ॐ कारवेद्यः पुरुषः पुराणो
बुद्धेश्च साक्षी निखिलस्य जन्तोः ।
यो वेत्ति सर्वं न च यस्य वेत्ता
परात्मरूपो भुवि रामकृष्णः ॥

*Omkāra-vedyaḥ puruṣaḥ purāṇo*
*buddheś ca sākṣī nikhilasya jantoḥ* |
*yo vetti sarvaṁ na ca yasya vettā*
*parātma-rūpo bhuvi Rāmakṛṣṇaḥ* ||

Thou art the Primeval Being sought to be known through the Omkāra.
In all creatures Thou art the witness of their self-conscious intelligence.
Thou knowest all, but there is none that knows Thee.
Thou, Rāmakṛṣṇa, art verily the Supreme Self manifest as the Lord incarnate on the earth.

*2*

न वेदगम्यो न च योगगम्यो
ध्यानैर्न जापैर्न तपोभिरुग्रैः ।

ज्ञेयः कदापीह ततोऽवतीर्णो
दयानिधे त्वं भुवि रामकृष्णः ॥

*Na veda-gamyo na ca yoga-gamyo*
*dhyānair na jāpair na tapobhir ugraiḥ* |
*jñeyaḥ kadāpī'ha tato'vatīrṇo*
*dayānidhe tvaṁ bhuvi Rāmakṛṣṇaḥ* ||

Thou art unattainable through the Veda or by Yoga;
Neither by meditation, nor by Japa, nor by stern austerity canst Thou ever be known.
Therefore hast Thou, the fountain-head of mercy,
Taken embodiment as Rāmakṛṣṇa, on earth.

*3*

मोक्षस्वरूपं तव धाम नित्यं
यथा तदाप्नोति विशुद्धचित्तः ।
तथोपदेष्टाऽखिलतत्त्ववेत्ता
त्वं विश्वधाता भुवि रामकृष्णः ।

*Mokṣa-svarūpaṁ tava dhāma nityaṁ*
*yathā tad āpnoti viśuddha-cittaḥ* |
*tatho'padeṣṭ'ākhila tattva-vettā*
*tvaṁ viśva-dhātā bhuvi Rāmakṛṣṇaḥ* ||

The condition of Mokṣa is Thy eternal Status.
The way how the pure-minded could attain it
Was shown by Thee, the knower of all Truth, through Thy instructions.

Thou Rāmakṛṣṇa, art thus the support of the countless
beings of the world.

*4*

भक्तेस्तथा शुद्धज्ञानस्य मार्गौ
प्रदर्शितौ द्वौ भवमुक्तिहेतू ।
तयोर्गतानां ध्रुवनायकोऽसि
त्वं मोक्षसेतुर्भुवि रामकृष्णः ।

*Bhakteś tathā śuddha-jñānasya mārgau*
*pradarśitau dvau bhava-mukti-hetū* |
*tayor gatānāṁ dhruva-nāyako'si*
*tvaṁ mokṣa-setur bhuvi Rāmakṛṣṇaḥ* ||

There are the two paths declared as leading to liberation—
The path of Bhakti and the path of pure knowledge.
Being the guide and leader of aspirants treading both
these paths,
Thou, Rāmakṛṣṇa, art verily the bridge to cross over to
the shores of liberation.

*5*

गतिस्त्वमेका जगतां जडानां
पुरा विसृष्टेश्चिदखण्डरूपः ।
तद्वल्लये स्या अधुनासि तद्वत्
त्वमादिदेवो भुवि रामकृष्णः ॥

*Gatis tvam ekā jagatāṁ jaḍānāṁ*
*purā visṛṣṭeś cid akhaṇḍa-rūpaḥ* |
*tadval laye syā adhunāsi tadvat*
*tvam ādi-devo bhuvi Rāmakṛṣṇaḥ* ||

Thou, the sole meaning of the otherwise insentient universe,
Didst exist as the undivided Existence and Consciousness even before creation;
Thou shalt exist even after all the creation has passed into dissolution.
But lo! Thou art the same undivided Existence when this creation subsists too.
Thou art verily that Original Being manifest on earth as Rāmakṛṣṇa.

*6*

वर्णाश्रमाचार - विहीन-शान्ताः
संन्यासिनो ज्ञानविधूतचित्ताः ।
ध्यायन्ति यं नित्यमभेददृष्ट्या
स एव हि त्वं भुवि रामकृष्णः ॥

*Varṇ'āśram'ācāra vihīna śāntāḥ*
*saṁnyāsino jñāna-vidhūta-cittāḥ* |
*dhyāyanti yaṁ nityam abheda-dṛṣṭyā*
*sa eva hi tvaṁ bhuvi Rāmakṛṣṇaḥ* ||

He on whom the Sannyāsins who have transcended the social rules and regulations,-
And who have attained to calmness and mental purity generated by knowledge —
The Being on whom such holy men meditate as Non-dual Consciousness —
That verily art Thou, Rāmakṛṣṇa, manifest on earth.

7

तेजोमयं दर्शयसि स्वरूपं
कोशान्तरस्थं परमार्थतत्त्वम् ।
संस्पर्शमात्रेण नृणां समाधिं
विधाय सद्यो भुवि रामकृष्णः ॥

*Tejomayaṁ darśayasi svarūpaṁ*
*koś'āntarasthaṁ paramārtha-tattvam* |
*saṁsparśa-mātreṇa nṛṇāṁ samādhiṁ*
*vidhāya sadyo bhuvi Rāmakṛṣṇaḥ* ||

Who inducing Samādhi in aspirants by his mere touch,
Revealed to them the Supreme Truth,
Thy real nature as Luminous Consciousness in the innermost core of the five Kośas —
That Supreme Spirit art Thou, Rāmakṛṣṇa, manifest on earth.

8

रागादिशून्यां तव सौम्यमूर्तिं
दृष्ट्वा पुनश्चात्र न जन्मभाजः ।
स्थाने यदादाय विशुद्धसत्त्व-
मिहावतीर्णो भुवि रामकृष्णः ॥

*Rāgādi-śūnyāṁ tava saumya-mūrtiṁ*
*dṛṣṭvā punaś cā'tra na janma-bhājaḥ* |
*sthāne yad ādāya viśuddha-sattvaṁ*
*ihāvatīrṇo bhuvi Rāmakṛṣṇaḥ* ||

Seeing Thy gentle form which is constituted of pure Sattva,
And which is free from the contamination of passions and attachments,
Man attains to that Status from which there is no return.
Thou hast for this purpose manifested Thyself as Rāmakṛṣṇa on earth.

*9*

महाविचित्रं महदादिकार्यं
लब्ध्वाप्यधिष्ठानमनाद्यनन्तम् ।
करोति नित्या प्रकृतिस्तवाद्या
तद्ब्रह्म सच्चिद् भुवि रामकृष्णः ॥

*Mahā vicitraṁ mahad-ādi kāryaṁ*
***labdhv'āpy'adhiṣṭhānam anādyanantam***
*karoti nityā prakṛtis'tav'ādyā*
*tad-brahma sac cid bhuvi Rāmakṛṣṇaḥ* ||

Obtaining Thee, the beginningless and endless Being, as support,
The Prakṛti, which is eternal and the cause of all causes,
Evolves all this wonderful universe constituted of categories beginning with Mahat.
That Brahman, the Being-Consciousness, Thou art manifest on earth as Rāmakṛṣṇa.

*10*

कृशाणुवत् तापविदग्धचित्ताः
संसारिणः शान्तिनिकेतनं त्वाम् ।
संप्राप्य शान्ता हि भवन्ति तेषां
त्वं शान्तिदाता भुवि रामकृष्णः ॥

*Kṛśāṇuvat tāpa-vidagdha-cittāḥ*
*saṁsāriṇaḥ śānti-niketanam tvām |*
*samprāpya śāntā hi bhavanti teṣāṁ*
*tvaṁ śānti-dātā bhuvi Rāmakṛṣṇaḥ ||*

Thou art the haven of peace,
To men with minds burning in the fiery ordeal of Saṁsāra.
Thy very proximity pacifies their restless mind.
As the bestower of peace hast Thou manifested on earth as Rāmakṛṣṇa.

*11*

षडङ्गयोगो न यतः सुसाध्यो
ज्ञानाधिकारी सुलभो न यस्मात् ।
गरीयसी भक्तिरतः कलौ स्यात्
तद् ज्ञापकस्त्वं भुवि रामकृष्णः ॥

*Ṣaḍaṅga-yogo na yataḥ susādhyo*
*jñān'ādhikārī sulabho na yasmāt |*
*garīyasī bhaktirataḥ kalau syāt*
*tad jñāpakas tvaṁ bhuvi Rāmakṛṣṇaḥ ||*

The eight-limbed Yoga of Patañjali is difficult to practise,
And aspirants competent to practise the discipline of knowledge are rare.
So, in this age of Kali the path of Bhakti is of special importance.
And to preach that hast Thou manifested on earth as Rāmakṛṣṇa.

*12*

नाकादिलोकं सुखदञ्च दिव्यं
सुरम्यमैश्वर्यमहं न याचे ।
हृदासने त्वं कृपया सदा वै
वसेति याचे भुवि रामकृष्णः ॥

*Nākādi-lokaṁ sukhadaṁ ca divyam*
*suramyam aiśvaryam aham na yāce* .|
*hṛdāsane tvaṁ kṛpayā sadā vai*
*vase'ti yāce bhuvi Rāmakṛṣṇaḥ* ||

Neither the higher realms yielding heavenly enjoyments,
Nor vast wealth on earth do I pray for.
Mayest Thou graciously take Thy seat in my heart —
Such is my prayer to Thee manifested on earth Rāmakṛṣṇa.

*13*

यं ब्रह्म विष्णू गिरिशश्च देवाः
ध्यायन्ति गायन्ति नमन्ति नित्यम् ।

तैः प्रार्थितस्तस्य परावतारो
द्विबाहुधारी भुवि रामकृष्णः ॥

*Yaṁ Brahma-Viṣṇū Giriśaś ca devāḥ*
*dhyāyanti gāyanti namanti nityam* |
*taiḥ prārthitas tasya parāvatāro*
*dvibāhu-dhārī bhuvi Rāmakṛṣṇaḥ* ||

Brahmā, Viṣṇu and Śiva the Lord of mountains
Meditate on, sing about, and do prostration to Thee at all times.
At their earnest prayer hast Thou come as the Supreme Incarnate,
Manifesting on earth in a human form as Rāmakṛṣṇa.

*14*

वन्दे जगद्बीजमखण्डमेकं
वन्दे सुरैः सेवितपादपीठम् ।
वन्दे भवेशं भवरोगवैद्यं
तमेव वन्दे भुवि रामकृष्णम् ॥

*Vande jagad-bījam akhaṇḍam ekaṁ*
*vande suraiḥ sevita pāda-piṭham* |
*vande bhaveśaṁ bhava-roga-vaidyaṁ*
*tam eva vande bhuvi Rāmakṛṣṇaḥ* ||

Salutations to the Supreme Cause, the Indivisible and the One without a second,

Salutations to the One whose foot-stool is the object of worship for all Divinities,
Salutations to the Master of this world of change and the physician of worldly miseries.
Him I adore who has manifested on earth as Rāmakṛṣṇa.

*15*

रामकृष्णं चिदानन्दं यः स्तौति भक्तिमान् सदा ।
तस्य चित्तं भवेच्छुध्दं तत्त्वज्ञानं स्वयं ततः ॥

***Rāmakṛṣṇaṁ cidānandaṁ yaḥ stauti bhaktimān sadā |***
***tasya cittaṁ bhavec chuddhaṁ tattva-jñānam svayam tataḥ ||***

Whoever adores Rāmakṛṣṇa, the Bliss-Consciousness, with devotion always,
His mind becomes pure, and he gains the knowledge of truth without any other aid.

# ŚRĪ RĀMAKṚṢṆĀ' ṢṬAKAM
## By Swāmī Abhedānanda

*1*

विश्वस्य धाता पुरुषस्त्वमाद्यो -
ऽव्यक्तेन रूपेण ततं त्वयेदम् ।
हे रामकृष्ण त्वयि भक्तिहीने
कृपाकटाक्षं कुरु देव नित्यम् ॥

*Viśvasya dhātā puruṣas tvam ādyo'-*
*vyaktena rūpeṇa tataṁ tvay'edam* |
*he Rāmakṛṣṇa tvayi bhakti-hīne*
*kṛpā-kaṭākṣaṁ kuru deva nityam* ||

Thou art the Ruler of the Worlds, and the Primordial Being,
By whose imperceptible form all this is pervaded.
O Rāmakṛṣṇa! Bestow Thy merciful glance on me, Thy faithless child.

*2*

त्वं पासि विश्वं सृजसि त्वमेव
त्वमादिदेवो विनिहंसि सर्वम् ।
हे रामकृष्ण त्वयि भक्तिहीने
कृपाकटाक्षं कुरु देव नित्यम् ॥

*Tvam pāsi viśvaṁ sṛjasi tvam eva*
*tvam ādidevo vinihaṁsi sarvam* |
*he Rāmakṛṣṇa tvayi bhakti-hīne*
*kṛpā-kaṭākṣaṁ kuru deva nityam* ||

Thou art the protector of the world and also its creator,
Thou, the Original Being, destroyest it too.
O Rāmakṛṣṇa! Bestow Thy merciful glance on me, Thy faithless child.

*3*

मायां समाश्रित्य करोषि लीलां
भक्तान् समुद्धर्त्तुमनन्तमूर्तिः ।
हे रामकृष्ण त्वयि भक्तिहीने
कृपाकटाक्षं कुरु देव नित्यम् ॥

*Māyāṁ samāśritya karoṣi līlām*
*bhaktān samuddharttum ananta mūrtiḥ* |
*he Rāmakṛṣṇa tvayi bhakti-hīne*
*kṛpā-kaṭākṣaṁ kuru deva nityam* ||

The Limitless Being that Thou art, Thou dost, in order to redeem Thy devotees,
Indulge in Thy play of redemption, assuming limitation by Thy power of Māyā.
O Rāmakṛṣṇa! Bestow Thy merciful glance on me, Thy faithless child.

*4*

विधृत्य रूपं नरवत्त्वया वै
विज्ञापितो धर्म इहाति गुह्यः ।
हे रामकृष्ण त्वयि भक्तिहीने
कृपाकटाक्षं कुरु देव नित्यम् ।

*Vidhṛtya rūpaṁ naravat tvayā vai*
*vijñāpito dharma ih'ātiguhyaḥ* |
*he Rāmakṛṣṇa tvayi bhakti-hīne*
*kṛpā-kaṭākṣaṁ kuru deva nityam* ||

Assuming a form that was in appearance human,
Thou dost proclaim the sacred Law, a mystery to men in ignorance,
O Rāmakṛṣṇa! Bestow Thy merciful glance on me, Thy faithless child.

*5*

तपोऽथ ते त्यागमदृष्टपूर्वं
दृष्ट्वा नमस्यन्ति कथं न विज्ञाः ।
हे रामकृष्ण त्वयि भक्तिहीने
कृपाकटाक्षं कुरु देव नित्यम् ॥

*Tapo'tha te tyāgam adṛṣṭa-pūrvam*
*dṛṣṭvā namasyanti kathaṁ na vijñāḥ* |
*he Rāmakṛṣṇa tvayi bhakti-hīne*
*kṛpā-kaṭākṣaṁ kuru deva nityam* ||

Unparalleled anywhere, at any time, is Thy practice of austerity and renunciation;
No man of wisdom can, on seeing Thy example, help bending his head to Thee in salutation.
O Rāmakṛṣṇa! Bestow Thy merciful glance on me, Thy faithless child.

*6*

श्रुत्वात्र ते नाम भवन्ति भक्ताः
दृष्ट्वा वयं त्वां न तु भक्तियुक्ताः ।
हे रामकृष्ण त्वयि भक्तिहीने
कृपाकटाक्षं कुरु देव नित्यम् ॥

*Śrutv'ātra te nāma bhavanti bhaktāḥ*
*dṛṣṭvā vayaṁ tvāṁ na tu bhakti-yuktāḥ |*
*he Rāmakṛṣṇa tvayi bhakti-hīne*
*kṛpā-kaṭākṣaṁ kuru deva nityam ||*

Merely hearing Thy name men become devoted to Thee,
But alas! Even seeing Thee we have not developed true devotion.
O Rāmakṛṣṇa! Bestow Thy merciful glance on me, Thy faithless child.

सत्यं विभुं शान्तमनादिरूपं
प्रसादये त्वामजमन्तशून्यम् ।
हे रामकृष्ण त्वयि भक्तिहीने
कृपाकटाक्षं कुरु देव नित्यम् ॥

*Satyaṁ vibhuṁ śāntam anādi-rūpam*
*prasādaye tvām ajam anta-śūnyam* |
*he Rāmakṛṣṇa tvayi bhakti-hīne*
*kṛpā-kaṭākṣaṁ kuru deva nityam* ||

Thou art the true, the good, the peaceful, the unborn and Thy being is without a beginning and an end.
O Rāmakṛṣṇa! Bestow Thy merciful glance on me, Thy faithless child.

*8*

जानामि तत्त्वं न हि देशिकेन्द्र
किं ते स्वरूपं किमु भावजातम् ।
हे रामकृष्ण त्वयि भक्तिहीने
कृपाकटाक्षं कुरु देव नित्यम् ॥

*Jānāmi tatvaṁ na hi deśikendra*
*kiṁ te svarūpaṁ kimu bhāva-jātam* |
*he Rāmakṛṣṇa tvayi bhakti-hīne*
*kṛpā-kaṭākṣaṁ kuru deva nityam* ||

I know not the truth about Thee, O World - Teacher,
Know not Thy true form, nor about Thy numerous manifestations.
O Rāmakṛṣṇa! Bestow Thy merciful glance on me, Thy faithless child.

## SRI RĀMAKṚṢṆA GUṆĀMṚTAM

By Swāmī Abhedānanda

*1*

न जानेऽन्यद्विना देवं रामकृष्णं कदाचन ।
यथाऽर्भको न जानाति किञ्चिद्धि मातरं विना ॥

*Na jāne'nyad vinā devam Rāmakṛṣṇaṁ kadācana |*
*yath'ārbhako na jānāti kiñcidd hi mātaraṁ vinā ||*

Other than Rāmakṛṣṇa, no Deity is known to us,
Just as an infant knows none but its mother.

*2*

कदा योगी कदा भोगी कदा वा ज्ञानवित्तमः ।
कदा भक्तः कदा शाक्तो वैष्णवश्चापि वा कदा ॥

*Kadā yogī kadā bhogī kadā vā jñāna-vittamaḥ |*
*kadā bhaktaḥ kadā śākto vaiṣṇavaś c'āpi vā kadā ||*

Sometimes a Yogi, sometimes a Bhogi (enjoyer), and sometimes a knowing one par excellence,
He appeared in turn as a Bhakta — as a votary of Śakti, or at times, of Viṣṇu too.

*3*

महाभावे कदा मत्तः प्रेमविह्वलमानसः ।
समाधौ वा कदा तिष्ठन् निर्विकल्पकसंज्ञके ॥

*Mahābhāve kadā mattaḥ prema-vihvala-mānasaḥ |*
*samādhau vā kadā tiṣṭhan nirvikalpaka - saṁjñake ||*

Caught up at times in the Mahābhāva, he appeared like one overpowered by love,
While at others, he was found deeply immersed in the transcendent state of Nirvikalpa consciousness.

*4*

पूर्णब्रह्म स्वरूपेण राजते यो महेश्वरः ।
परानन्दात्मनस्तस्य चैतन्यघनरूपिणः ॥

*Pūrṇa-brahma-svarūpeṇa rājate yo maheśvaraḥ |*
*parānand' ātmanas tasya caitanya-ghana-rūpiṇaḥ ||*

Of that Supreme Lord and perfect manifestation of Brahman,
Of Him the soul of transcendent Bliss and a concrete condensation of Pure Consciousness—

*5*

लीलारूपहरेरेवं भक्तार्थं देहधारिणः ।
रामकृष्णस्वरूपस्य नानाभावसमन्वितान् ॥

*Līlārūpa-harer evaṁ bhakt'ārthaṁ deha-dhāriṇaḥ* |
*Rāmakṛṣṇa-svarūpasya nānā-bhāva-samanvitān* ||

Of Him Śrī Hari who has assumed a form for the sake of devotees
As Rāmakṛṣṇa combining in Himself innumerable divine moods —

*6*

अशेषांश्च गुणान् दृष्ट्वा संश्रुत्य च पुनः पुनः ।
कीदृशो रामकृष्णोऽस्ति सच्चिदानन्दविग्रहः ।
ज्ञातुं सम्यक् स्थिरीकर्तुं कः शक्नोत्यत्र मानवः ॥

*Aśeṣāṁś ca guṇān dṛṣṭvā saṁśrutya ca punaḥ punaḥ* |
*kīdṛśo Rāmakṛṣṇ'osti sac-cid-ānanda-vigrahaḥ* |
*jñātum samyak sthirīkartuṁ kaḥ śaknoty atra mānavaḥ* ||

Who is the man that can form an estimate of His greatness and determine his identity,
After making a total study time and again of His glorious traits and form of Existence–Knowledge–Bliss?

*7*

यदि त्वं कृपया देव ज्ञापयस्यन्तरात्मनि ।
यद्रूपं यं स्वभावञ्च धारयस्यात्ममायया ॥

*Yadi tvaṁ kṛpayā deva jñāpayasy antarātmani* |
*yad rūpam yaṁ svabhāvam ca dhārayasy ātma-māyayā* ||

It is only if Thou, O Lord, deignest to reveal Thy form in the innermost heart,
Only then can one understand a bit of the form and character that Thou assumest with the help of Thy inherent Power;

8

तदा तत्तद्विजानाति त्वद्भक्तो भक्तवत्सल ।
समाप्नोति परां शान्तिं यल्लाभादमृतो भवेत् ॥

*Tadā tat tad vijānati tvad-bhakto bhakta-vatsala* |
*samāpnoti paraṁ śāntim yal lābhād amṛto bhavet* ||

Then only, O lover of devotees, shall they, Thy dependants, know the truth about Thee,
And attain the Supreme Peace, gaining which one becomes Immortal.

9

तत्त्वं देव न जानामि रामकृष्ण तव प्रभो ।
यादृशोऽसि कृपासिन्धो तादृशाय नमो नमः ॥

*Tattvaṁ deva na jānāmi Rāmakṛṣṇa tava prabho* |
*yādṛśo'si kṛpāsindho tādṛśāya namo namaḥ* ||

O Rāmakṛṣṇa, Thou all-mighty Lord! though I know not the ultimate truth about Thee,
Still I salute again and again that aspect of Thine that Thou, Ocean of mercy, hast deigned to reveal.

## SRI RĀMAKṚṢṆA- STOTRA-DAŚAKAM
### By Swāmī Virajānanda

*1*

ब्रह्म-रूपमादि-मध्य-शेष-सर्व-भासकं
भाव-षट्क-हीनरूप नित्य-सत्यमद्वयम् ।
वाङ्मनोऽति-गोचरञ्च नेति-नेति-भावितं
तं नमामि देव-देव-रामकृष्णमीश्वरम् ॥

*Brahma-rūpam ādi-madhya-śeṣa-sarva-bhāsakam*
*bhāva-ṣaṭka-hīnarūpa nitya-satyam-advayam* |
*vāṅmano'ti-gocarañ ca neti-neti bhāvitaṁ*
*taṁ namāmi deva-deva Rāmakṛṣṇam īśvaram* ||

He who is of the form of Brahman, existing as the Consciousness that reveals everything included in the cosmic process as its beginning, the middle and the end,

He who is devoid of the six mutations to which all are subject and who is the Non-dual Reality which eternally exists as the Truth,

He who is beyond the ken of mind and speech but implied as the positive background of the ultimate negation 'Neti Neti' —

To Him, Rāmakṛṣṇa, the Lord Supreme and the source of all Divinities, my salutations!

*2*

आदितेय भीहरं सुरारि-दैत्य-नाशकम्
साधु-शिष्ट-कामदं मही-सुभार-हारकम् ।
स्वात्म-रूप-तत्त्वकं युगे युगे च दर्शितं
तं नमामि देव-देवरामकृष्णमीश्वरम् ।

*Āditeya-bhīharam surāri-daitya-nāśakam*
*sādhu-śiṣṭa-kāmadaṁ mahī-subhāra-hārakam* |
*svātma-rūpa-tattvakaṁ yuge yuge ca darśitam*
*taṁ namāmi deva-deva Rāmakṛṣṇam īśvaram* ||

He who is the destroyer of fear from all evil forces and the effacer of the titanic being of scepticism that destroys all goodness in man,
He who is the fulfiller of the aspirations of all the good and holy men and the remover of the world's heavy burden of evil,
He who is the manifestation of the Universal Spirit present in all, and the one who comes from age to age as the Divine Incarnate —
To Him, Rāmakṛṣṇa, the Lord Supreme and the source of all Divinities, my salutation!

3

सर्व-भूत-सर्ग-कर्म-सूत्र-बन्ध-कारणं
ज्ञान-कर्म-पाप-पुण्य-तारतम्य-साधनम् ।
बुद्धि-वास-साक्षि-रूप-सर्व -कर्म भासनं
तं नमामि देव-देवरामकृष्णमीश्वरम् ।

*Sarva-bhūta-sarga-karma-sūtra - bandha-kāraṇam*
*jñāna-karma-pāpa-puṇya-tāratamya sādhanam |*
*buddhi-vāsa-sākṣi-rūpa-sarva-karma-bhāsanam*
*taṁ namāmi deva-deva-Rāmakṛṣṇam iśvaram ||*

The wielder of the string of Karma that regulates the origin and the evolution of all beings,
The goal that is attained by the neutralisation of Karma by Jñāna, and of Pāpa (demerit) by Purity (merit),
The witness residing in the intellect of all and making all actions possible —
To Him, Rāmakṛṣṇa, the Lord Supreme and the source of all Divinities, my salutations!

*4*

सर्व-जीव-पाप-नाश-कारणं भवेश्वरं
स्वीकृतज्ञगर्भवास देह पाशमीदृशम् ।
स्थापितं स्व-लीलया च येन दिव्य जीवनं
तं नमामि देव-देवरामकृष्णमीश्वरम् ।

*Sarva-jīva-pāpa-nāśa-kāraṇaṁ-bhaveśvaram*
*svīkṛtañ ca garbhavāsa-deha-pāśam īdṛśam* |
*sthāpitaṁ sva-līlayā ca yena divya jīvanam*
*taṁ namāmi deva-deva Rāmakṛṣṇam īśvaram* ||

The destroyer of the sins of all Jivas and the master presiding over the cycle of transmigratory existence,
The one who for this purpose had willingly adopted the bondage and travails of bodily existence
And who as the Incarnate demonstrated the Life Divine as an act of play —
To Him, Rāmakṛṣṇa, the Lord Supreme and the source of all Divinities, my salutations!

*5*

तुल्य-लोष्ट-काञ्चनञ्च हेयनेय-धीगतम्
स्त्रीषु-नित्य-मातृरूप-शक्ति-भाव-भावुकम् ।
ज्ञान-भक्ति-भुक्ति-मुक्ति-शुद्धबुद्धि-दायकं
तं नमामि देव-देवरामकृष्णमीश्वरम् ।

*Tulya loṣṭa-kāñcanañ ca heya-ṇeya-dhīgatam*
*strīṣu nitya-mātṛ-rūpa-śakti-bhāva-bhāvukam* |
*jñāna-bhakti-bhukti-mukti-śuddha-buddhi-dāyakaṁ*
*taṁ namāmi deva-deva Rāmakṛṣṇam īśvaram* ||

He who mentally equated gold and a clod of earth as equal non-values in the path of God-realisation and was indifferent to both alike,

Who looked upon all women as manifestations of Śakti, the Universal Mother Divine,
And who bestowed on seekers knowledge and devotion, liberation and enjoyment, besides purity of mind —
To Him, Rāmakṛṣṇa, the Lord Supreme and the source of all Divinities, my salutations!

*6*

सर्व-धर्म-गम्य-मूल-सत्य-तत्त्व-देशकं
सिद्ध-सर्व-सम्प्रदाय साम्प्रदाय-वर्जितम् ।
सर्व-शास्त्र-मर्मदर्शि सर्वविन्निरक्षरं
तं नमामि देव-देवरामकृष्णमीश्वरम् ।

*Sarva-dharma-gamya-mūla-satya-ṭattva-deśakam*
*siddha-sarva-sampradāya-sāmpradāya-varjitam* |
*sarva-śāstra-marma-darśi sarva-vin nirakṣaraṁ*
*taṁ namāmi deva-deva Rāmakṛṣṇam īśvaram* ||

He who preached the one Eternal Truth underlying all religions,
Who attained realisation through all faiths but never identified himself exclusively with any particular faith,
And who knew the essence of all scriptures and was all-knowing without being book-learned at all —
To Him, Rāmakṛṣṇa, the Lord Supreme and the source of all Divinities, my salutations!

चारुदर्श-कालिका-सुगीत-चारु-गायकं
कीर्त्तनेषु मत्तवच्च नित्य-भाव-विह्वलम् ।
सूपदेश-दायकं हि शोक-ताप-वारक
तं नमामि देव-देव रामकृष्णमीश्वरम् ॥

*Cārudarśa-kālikā-sugīta-cāru-gāyakam*
*kīrtaneṣu-matta-vac ca nitya-bhāva-vihvalam* ।
*sūpadeśa-dāyakaṁ hi śoka-tāpa-vārakaṁ*
*taṁ namāmi deva-deva Rāmakṛṣṇam īśvaram* ॥

Handsome in appearance and rapturous in singing
inspiring songs on Kālī,
Inebriated on hearing songs on the Lord and ever
stirred by various Divine moods (Bhāvas),
And ever engaged in giving spiritual instructions and
in assuaging the grief of the sorrow-stricken —
To Him, Rāmakṛṣṇa, the Lord Supreme and the source
of all Divinities, my salutations!

*8*

पाद-पद्म-तत्त्व-बोध-शान्ति-सौख्य दायक
सक्त-चित्त-भक्त-सूनु-नित्यवित्त-वर्धनम् ।
दंभि-दर्प-दारणन्तु निर्भयं जगद्गुरुं
तं नमामि देव-देवरामकृष्णमीश्वरम् ॥

*Pāda-padma-tattva-bodha-śānti-saukhya-dāyakaṁ*
***sakta-citta-bhakta-sūnu-nityavitta-vardhanam*** |
*dambhi-darpa-dāraṇam tu nirbhayaṁ jagadguruṁ*
*taṁ namāmi deva-deva Ramakṛṣṇam īśvaram* ||

He the touch of whose lotus feet gave Enlightenment and the bliss of Peace,
He who enhanced the spiritual well-being of even such devotee-children as went to Him with worldly desires,
He who could see through the professions of the hypocritical and humble their pride,
The fearless one embodied as the World-Teacher —
To Him, Rāmakṛṣṇa, the Lord Supreme and the source of all Divinities, my salutations!

*9*

पञ्चवर्ष-बाल-भाव-युक्त-हंस-रूपिणं
सर्व-लोक-रञ्जनं भवाब्धि-सङ्ग-भञ्जनम् ।
शान्ति-सौख्य-सद्म जीव-जन्म-भीति-नाशनं
तं नमामि देव-देवरामकृष्णमीश्वरम् ।

*Pañca-varṣa-bāla-bhāva-yukta-haṁsa-rūpiṇam*
*sarva-loka-rañjanaṁ bhavābdhi-saṅga-bhañjanam* |
***śānti-saukhya-sadma-jīva-janma-bhīti-nāśanam***
*taṁ namāmi deva-deva Rāmakṛṣṇam īśvaram* ||

**A Paramahaṁsa whose nature was as innocent as of a boy of five years,**

One who delighted the whole world and snapped people's attachment for worldly life,
The abode of all bliss and peace, and the destroyer of **the Jīva's fear of birth and death —**
To Him, Rāmakṛṣṇa, the Lord Supreme and the source of all Divinities, my salutations!

*10*

धर्महानहारकं त्वधर्मकर्म वारकं
लोकधर्म-चारणञ्च सर्वधर्म-कोविदम् ।
त्यागि-गेहि-सेव्य-नित्य-पावनाङ्घ्रि-पङ्कजं
तं नमामि देव-देवरामकृष्णमीश्वरम् ॥

***Dharma-hāna-hārakam tv'adharma-karma vārakam***
*loka-dharma cāraṇañ ca sarvadharma-kovidam* |
*tyāgi-gehi-sevya-nitya-pāvanāṅghri-paṅkajam*
*taṁ namāmi deva-deva Rāmakṛṣṇam īśvaram* ||

He who arrested the decay of Dharma and stopped the growth of Adharma,
He who appeared to follow the Dharma of the world but was in truth the master of all Dharmas,
He whose feet were served alike both by world-renouncing ascetics and householders living in the world —
To Him, Rāmakṛṣṇa, the Lord Supreme and the source of all Divinities, my salutations!

*11*

स्तोत्र-शून्य-सोमकं सदेश भाव व्यञ्जकं
नित्य पाठकस्य वै विपत्ति-पुञ्ज-नाशकम् ।

स्यात्कदापि जाप-याग-योग-भोग-सौलभं
दुर्लभन्तु रामकृष्ण-राग-भक्ति-भावनम् ॥

*Stotra-śūnya-somakaṁ sadeśa-bhāva-vyañjakaṁ*
*nitya-pāṭhakasya vai vipatti-puñja-nāśakam* |
*syāt-kadāpi jāpa-yāga-yoga-bhoga-saulabhaṁ*
*durlabhaṁ tu Rāmakṛṣṇa rāga-bhakti-bhāvanam*

This is the ten-versed hymn revealing the greatness of Śrī Rāmakṛṣṇa, the Lord Everlasting,
The daily study of which is a safeguard against all threatening dangers.
It is comparatively easy to perform Japa, Yāga and Yoga, and to have Bhoga too,
But rare it is to be endowed with supreme loving devotion to Rāmakṛṣṇa!

*12*

इति श्रीविरजानन्द-रचितं भक्ति-साधकम् ।
स्तव-सारं समाप्तं वै श्रीरामकृष्ण-तूणकम् ॥

*Iti śrī Virajānanda racitaṁ bhakti-sādhakaṁ* |
*stava-sāram samāptaṁ vai Śrī Rāmakṛṣṇa tūṇakam* ||

Thus ends the hymn composed by Virajānanda on Śri Rāmakṛṣṇa in Tūṇaka metre, as an aid to the development of devotion.

## SRI RĀMAKṚṢṆ' ĀṢṬOTTARAŚATA NĀMĀVALIḤ

### By Swāmī Vimalānanda

*1*

ॐ श्री चन्द्रमणीदेवी क्षुदिरामात्मजन्मने
अकर्मायात्तदेहाय धर्मसंस्थितिहेतवे ॥

*Oṁ Śrī Chandramaṇīdevī-Kṣudirām'ātma-janmane |.*
*akarmāy'ātta-dehāya dharma-saṁsthiti-hetave ||*

Om.. O Thou who took birth by the Holy Spirit in Candramaṇī Devi and Kṣudirāma!

O Thou whose embodiment was not the effect of Karma!

O Thou who was the cause of the survival of spirituality in the world!

2

रामकृष्णैकरूपाय मातृवात्सल्यभूमये
गदाधराय धीराय सर्वमानसहारिणे ॥

*Rāmakṛṣṇ'aika-rūpāya mātṛ-vātsalya-bhūmaye |*
*Gadādharāya dhīrāya sarva-mānasa-hāriṇe ||*

O Thou who art the same as He who came as Rāma and Kṛṣṇa,
O Thou the centre of Thy mother's affection!
**O Thou the Lord Gadādhara of Gayā incarnated as** Gadādhara!
O Thou who art established in the spiritual Self!
O Thou who attractest the minds of all!

3

सर्वानवद्यगात्राय सौम्यायामिततेजसे ।
शूद्राभिक्षान्नतृप्ताय पूर्णब्राह्मण्यमूर्त्तये ॥

*Sarv'ānavadya-gātrāya saumyāy'āmita-tejase* |
*śūdrā-bhikṣānna-tṛptāya pūrṇa-brāhmaṇya-mūrtaye* ||

O Thou with a flawless form!
O Thou endowed with a gentle nature!
O Thou of unabating splendour!
O Thou who didst deign to take alms from the depressed and the down-trodden!
O Thou who yet wert endowed with full Brāhmic splendour!

4

नाट्यगानविनोदाय पण्डितश्लाघ्यमेधसे ।
चित्रकेलिकलाकृष्टजनविस्मयहेतवे ।

*Nātya-gāna-vinodāya paṇḍita-ślāghya-medhase* |
*citra-keli-kal'ākṛṣṭa-jana-vismaya-hetave* ||

O Thou who didst delight to sing and act!
O Thou whose intelligence even in boyhood received the praise of scholars!
O Thou who didst astonish the people by Thy skill in fine arts!

5

वलाकालंकृताकाशसमीक्षणसमाधिने ।
नटवेषशिवोद्दीप्तशिवात्मैक्यानुभूतये ॥

*Valāk'ālaṁkṛt'ākāśa-samīkṣaṇa-samādhine* |
*naṭa-veṣa-śivod-dīpta-śivātm'aiky'ānubhūtaye* ||

O Thou who didst enter into Samādhi at the sight of the sombre sky, bespangled by a flight of white cranes!
O Thou who, on being dressed as Śiva, became stimulated into Śiva-consciousness and attained union with Śiva!

6

आजन्मपूर्णसिद्धाय साधनोल्फुल्लसिद्धये ।
अवधूतार्थकामाय पराविद्यैकलिप्सवे ॥

*Ājanma-pūrṇa-siddhāya sādhan'odphulla-siddhaye* |
*avadhūt'ārtha-kāmāya parā-vidyaika-lipsave* ||

O Thou who wert born perfect!
O Thou who through Sādhanas didst manifest that perfection!
O Thou who didst yearn to follow the Avadhūta's ideal!
**O Thou who wert devoted to Parāvidyā alone!**

7

स्वनुष्ठितस्वधर्माय सारदागृहमेधिने ।
स्वर्धूनीवारिनिर्धूतदक्षिणेश्वरवासिने ॥

***Svanuṣṭhita-svadharmāya sāradā-gṛha-medhine |***
*svardhūnī-vāri-nirdhūta-Dakṣiṇeśvara-vāsine ||*

O Thou who didst perform Thy Svadharma with devotion!
**O Thou who with Sāradā as Thy counterpart assumed the householder's state!**
**O Thou who didst take Thy residence at Dakṣineśvara, sanctified by the waters of the heavenly river Gaṅgā!**

8

राधागोविन्ददेवाय भवतारिण्युपासिने ।
दक्षिणाकालिकापूजाविस्मृताखिलकर्मणे ॥

***Rādhā-govinda-devāya bhava-tāriṇyupāsine |***
*dakṣinā-kālikā-pūjā-vismṛt'ākhila-karmaṇe ||*

O Thou! who performed the worship of Rādhā-Govinda!
O Thou who meditated on Bhavatāriṇī!
O Thou who forgot all steps of rituals in Thy absorption in the worship of Dakṣiṇā-Kālikā!

9

तपः समाधिसम्प्राप्तकालीदर्शनहर्षिणे ।
सर्वतन्त्रक्रियासाध्यसिध्युत्भासितवर्ष्मणे ॥

*Tapaḥ-samādhi-samprāpta-kālī-darśana-harṣiṇe* |
*sarva-tantra-kriyā-sādhya-siddhy'utbhāsita-varṣmaṇe* ||

O Thou who wert steeped in bliss by the vision of Kāli through austerities and Samādhi!
O Thou who shone resplendent by all the Siddhis open to one through the Tāntric rites!

10

स्ववधूषोडशीपादपूजाप्रणिहितात्मने ।
राधाभावमहत्वाय सीतावीक्षणमोदिने ॥

*Sva-vadhū-ṣoḍaśī-pāda-pūjā-praṇihit'ātmane* |
*Rādhā-bhāva-mahatvāya Sītā-vīkṣaṇa-modine* ||

O Thou who worshipped and saluted Thy own wife as the Goddess Ṣodaśi!
O Thou who manifested the glory of Rādha!
O Thou who wert delighted by the vision of Sītā!

11

आञ्जनेयात्मभूताय गौराङ्गस्फूर्तिमूर्तये ।
प्रत्यक्षितेशपुत्राय निबिरुपावलोकिने ॥

*Āñjaney'ātma-bhūtāya Gaurāṅga-sphūrti-mūrtaye |*
*pratyakṣite'eśa-putrāya Nibi-rūp'āvalokine ||*

O Thou who personated as Hanumān!
O Thou who wert the full embodiment of Gaurāṅga!
O Thou who saw Christ, the Son of God, with Thy eyes!
O Thou who had a vision of Nibi's form!

12

बालगोपालरूपाय हररूपविधारिणे ।
सर्वनारीशरीरस्थश्रीजगन्मातृदर्शिने ॥

*Bālagopāla-rūpāya Hara-rūpa-vidhāriṇe |*
*sarva-nārī-śarīrastha-śrī-jagan-mātṛ-darśine ||*

O Thou who appeared as Bāla - gopāla!
O Thou who took the form of Hara!
O Thou who realised the Mother of the Universe as residing in all female forms!

13

रासमणीमधुरादीष्टगुरुदैवतरूपिणे ।
शमादिषट्कयुक्ताय यतिधर्मस्वरूपिणे ॥

*Rāsmaṇī-Madhur'ād'īṣṭa-guru-daivata-rūpiṇe* |
*śamādi-ṣaṭka-yuktāya yati-dharma-svarūpiṇe* ||

O Thou who appeared both as the Chosen Deity and the Guru for Rāsmaṇi and Madhura!
O Thou who wert endowed with the six excellences beginning with tranquillity (Śama)!
O Thou who wert the very embodiment of the Dharma of the Sannyāsins!

14

दम्भाहंकारशून्याय वात्सल्यौदार्यवर्धये ।
कामक्रोधविहीनाय मार्दवार्जवशालिने ॥

*Daṁbh'āhaṁkāra-śūnyāya vātsaly'audārya-vardhaye* |
*kāma-krodha-vihīnāya mārdav'ārjava-śāline* ||

**O Thou who hadst no touch of hypocrisy and pride!**
O Thou who wert overflowing with love and benevolence!
O Thou who wert free from lust, anger and other passions!
O Thou who wert mild and pleasing in Thy nature, but straight-forward at the same time.

*15*

एषणात्रयमुक्ताय हेममृत्तुल्यदर्शिने ।
भगवत्भक्तधुर्याय गानमाधुर्यसिन्धवे ॥

*Eṣaṇā-traya-muktāya hema-mṛt-tulya-darśine* |
*bhagavat-bhakta-dhuryāya gāna-mādhurya-sindhave* ||

O Thou! who wert free from the threefold longings — the longing for wealth, for off-spring and for higher realms!
O Thou who looked upon gold and mud as alike in worth!
O Thou who wert the most noted among the devotees of the Lord!
O Thou whose devotional singing was a veritable ocean of Divine love!

*16*

स्थितप्रज्ञाय शुद्धाय लोकसंग्रहकारिणे ।
गुणातीताय शान्ताय सर्वतीर्थस्वरूपिणे ॥

***Sthita-prajñāya śuddhāya loka-saṁgraha-kāriṇe*** |
*guṇ'ātītāya śāntāya sarva-tīrtha-svarūpiṇe* ||

O Thou whose intellect was established in unwavering certitude!
O Thou of unsullied purity!
O Thou whose life was meant only for the good of the world!
O Thou who didst transcend the three Guṇas of Prakṛti!
O Thou who wert ever established in peace!
O Thou who wert the embodiment of all holy spots and objects!

*17*

अमानिने मानदाय पुण्यश्लोकाय योगिने ।
तोतापुरी-गुरुप्राप्त-ब्रह्मात्मैक्यानुभूतये ॥

*Amānine mānadāya puṇya-ślokāya yogine |*
*Totāpurī-guru-prāpta-brahm'ātm'aikay'ānubhūtaye ||*

O Thou who never sought honour for oneself from others!
O Thou who nevertheless showed respect to others!
O Thou who wert famous for holiness!
O Thou who wert a Yogin!
O Thou who under the instruction of the teacher Totāpurī, attained to oneness with Brahman!

*18*

सर्वभूतात्मभूताय सर्वभूतानुकम्पिने ।
सर्वानुस्यूतचिन्मात्रदर्शिनेऽमृतमूर्त्तये ॥

*Sarva-bhūt'ātma-bhūtāya sarva-bhūt'ānukampine |*
*sarv'ānusyūta-cinmātra-darśine'mṛta-mūrtaye ||*

O Thou who felt one with the spirit pervading all!
O Thou who felt sympathy for all!
O Thou who perceived all as the one Spirit pervading them!
O Thou whose Being is Immortality!

*19*

पुष्पशष्पनृपक्ष्यादिसर्वभूतान्तरात्मने ।
लोकशिक्षणदक्षाय जीवसेवाविधायिने ॥

*Puṣpa-śaṣpa-nṛ-pakṣyādi-sarva-bhūt'āntar'ātmane |*
*loka-śikṣaṇa-dakṣāya jīva-sevā-vidhāyine |*

O Thou who felt one in spirit with flowers, grass, men, birds, and all other creatures!
O Thou who wert highly competent in imparting instruction to men!
O Thou who preached the gospel of service of all Jīvas as temples of Divinity!

*20*

अपरोक्षीकृताशेष धर्मतत्त्वप्रकाशिने ।
गृहमेधिनिदर्शाय नैष्ठिकब्रह्मचारिणे ।

*Aparokṣī-kṛt'āśeṣa-dharma-tattva-prakāśine |*
*gṛha-medhi-nidarśāya naiṣṭhika-brahmacāriṇe ||*

O Thou who preached the truth of the scriptures out of Thy own realisation!
O Thou who wert an ideal for householders!
O Thou who at the same time wert a Brahmacārin observing unbroken continence!

21

विद्वद्वरेण्यपूज्याय केशवस्तुत्यकीर्तये ।
साधुषट्पदजुष्टाय वेदवेदान्तभानवे ॥

*Vidvad-vareṇya-pūjyāya Keśava-stutya-kīrtaye |*
*sādhu-ṣaṭpada-juṣṭāya veda-vedānta-bhānave ||*

O Thou who wert worshipped by the greatest of the Enlightened!
O Thou whose fame was spread by Keśava's writings!
O Thou who wert surrounded by pious devotees as honey bees gather round a blooming lotus!
O Thou who wert the luminous sun of the Vedas and the Vedānta!

22

गिरीशादिसमुद्धर्त्रे विवेकानन्दबन्धवे ।
ब्रह्मानन्दशिवानन्दाद्यन्तेवास्याश्रितांघ्रये ॥

*Girīś'ādi-samuddhartre Vivekānanda-bandhave|*
*Brahmānanda-Śivānand'ādy'ante-vāsy'āśrīt'āṅ-ghraye||*

O Thou who wert the saviour of Girīśa and others!
O Thou who had Vivekānanda as companion!
O Thou whose feet formed the shelter for disciples like Brahmānaṇda and Śivānaṇda!

*23*

आचण्डालवितीर्णस्वप्रेमपीयूषसम्पदे ।
दुराचारविघाताय सदाचारप्रवर्तिने ॥

*Acaṇḍāla-vitīrṇa-sva-prema-pīyuṣa-sampade|*
*durācāra-vighātāya sadācāra-pravartine||*

O Thou whose love extended to all up to the most depressed and the downtrodden!
O Thou who discouraged evil practices!
O Thou who encouraged high morality!

*24*

अष्टपाशविमुक्ताय कलिदोषापहारिणे ।
सर्वार्हणीयशीलाय देवायाभीष्टदायिने ॥

*Aṣṭapāśa-vimuktāya kali-doṣ'āpahāriṇe|*
*sarv'ārhaṇīya-śīlāya devāy'ābhīṣṭa-dāyine||*

O Thou who wert free from the eight bondages!
O Thou who eradicatest the evils of the Kali age!
O Thou who wert the possessor of all excellences!
O Thou the Divine Being,
O Thou the grantor of all that one prays for!

*25*

जन्ममृत्युजरातप्तजनविश्रान्तिभूमये ।
समाधिनिष्ठचित्ताय भक्तहृत्पद्मवासिने ॥

*Janma-mṛtyu-jarā-tapta-jana-viśrānti-bhūmaye|*
*samādhi-niṣṭha-cittāya bhakta-hṛt-padma-vāsine||*

O Thou who art the resting ground for those who are scorched by the fire of birth, death and old age!
O Thou whose mind was ever established in Samādhi!
O Thou who dwellest in the heart-lotus of devotees!

*26*

ज्ञानविज्ञानतृप्ताय ज्ञानविज्ञानदायिने ।
आत्मसंस्थाय सत्याय शरण्यगुणशालिने ।।

*Jñāna-vijñāna-tṛptāya jñāna-vijñāna-dāyine |*
*ātma-saṁsthāya satyāya śaraṇya-guṇa-śāline ||*

O Thou who art the fulness of Jñāna and Vijñāna!
O Thou who art the bestower of Jñāna and Vijñāna to devotees!
O Thou who art Thyself the Truth
O Thou who art the one endowed with all excellences
O Thou who art a shelter for all!

*27*

संसारकर्णधाराय संशयग्रन्थिभेदिने ।
अव्याजकरुणायात्म-दीपायानन्दमूर्तये ॥

*Saṁsāra-karṇadhārāya saṁśaya-granthi-bhedine |*
*avyāja-karuṇāy'ātma-dīpāy'ānanda-mūrtaye ||*

O Thou the Captain of the ship that takes the Jīvas across the ocean of Samsāra!
O Thou who snappest the knot of scepticism in the hearts of aspirants!
O Thou who art Mercy unalloyed and abounding!
O Thou who lightest the lamp of wisdom in the heart of aspirants!
O Thou who art the embodiment of Bliss!

*28*

सर्वदेवीस्वरूपाय सर्वदेवस्वरूपिणे ।
विरक्तिभक्तिनैर्मल्य-भूतिमंगलकारिणे ॥

*Sarvadevī-svarūpāya sarva-deva-svarūpiṇe|*
*virakti-bhakti-nairmalya-bhūti-maṅgala-kāriṇe ||*

O Thou the embodiment of all Devis!
O Thou who art all the Devas embodied as one!
O Thou who bringest into blossom renunciation, devotion and purity!
O Thou who art the bestower of all excellences in abundance.

*29*

भक्तहार्दतमोभेदिदिव्यजोतिःस्वरूपिणे ।
प्रपन्नत्राणदीक्षाय रामकृष्णाय ॐ नमः ॥

*Bhakta-hārda-tamo-bhedi-divya-jyotiḥ-svarūpiṇe* |
*prapanna-trāṇa-dīkṣāya Rāmakṛṣṇāya oṁ namaḥ* ||

O Thou who art the shatterer of the darkness of ignorance in the heart of devotees!
O Thou who art the light Divine!
O Thou who art vowed to give protection to all the ones who surrender !
O Thou who hast come as Rāmakṛṣṇa!
O salutation to Thee Om!

*30*

अष्टोत्तरशतं नाम्नां विमलानन्ददायकम् ।
गृणतां तुष्यताद्देवो रामकृष्णो जगदगुरुः ॥

*Aṣṭottara-śataṁ-nāmnāṁ vimalānanda-dāyakam* |
*gṛṇatāṁ tuṣyatād devo Rāmākṛṣṇo jagad-guruḥ* ||

This hymn of a hundred and eight names that bestows Vimalānanda (taintless bliss) and has been composed by Vimalānanda —
May Thou be pleased to accept it, O Lord, Thou Rāmakṛṣṇa the Teacher of the world!

# ŚRĪ SĀRADĀ DEVĪ STOTRAM

## By Swāmī Abhedānanda

*1*

प्रकृतिं परमामभयां वरदां नररूपधरां जनतापहराम् ।
शरणागत सेवक तोषकरीं प्रणमामि परां जननीं जगताम् ॥ १ ॥

*Prakṛtiṁ paramām abhayāṁ varadāṁ*
*nararūpa-dharāṁ janatāpa-harāṁ |*
*śaraṇāgata-sevaka-toṣa-karīṁ*
*praṇamāmi parāṁ jananīṁ jagatām. ||*

To the Divine Śakti (Power) embodied in a human form,
To the giver of boons and the asylum to those afflicted with fears,
To the redresser of man's miseries and the generator of joy in the hearts of devotees,
To Thee my salutations! O Supreme Being, Mother of the worlds!

2

गुणहीनसुतानपराधयुतान् कृपयाऽद्य समुद्धर मोहगतान् ।
तरणीं भवसागरपारकरीं प्रणमामि परां जननीं जगताम् ॥ २ ॥

*Guṇahīna sutān aparādhayutān*
*kṛpayā'dya samuddhara moha-gatān* |
*taraṇīm bhava-sāgara-pārakarīm*
*praṇamāmi parāṁ jananīm jagatām* ||

Redeem Thy children by Thy mercy — worthless, sinful and deluded though they be,
A veritable ship ferrying them across the ocean of Saṁsāra that Thou art.
To Thee my salutations, O Supreme Being, O Mother of the worlds!

*3*

विषयं कुसुमं परिहृत्य सदा चरणाम्बुरुहामृत शान्तिसुधाम् ।
पिब भृङ्ग मनो भवरोगहरां प्रणमामि परां जननीं जगताम् ॥ ३ ॥

*Viṣayaṁ kusumaṁ parihṛtya sadā*
*caraṇ'āmburuhāmṛta śānti-sudhām* |
*piba bhṛṅga-mano bhava-roga harāṁ*
*praṇamāmi parāṁ jananīṁ jagatām.* ||

Abandoning the flowers of worldly enjoyments, imbibe O honey-bee of my mind!
The nectar of the lotus of Mother's feet, the sure panacea for the disease of worldliness.
To Thee my salutations, O Supreme Being, O Mother of the worlds!

*4*

कृपां कुरु महादेवि सुतेषु प्रणतेषु च ।
चरणाश्रयदानेन कृपामयि नमोऽस्तुते ॥ ४ ॥

*Kṛpāṁ kuru mahādevi suteṣu praṇateṣu ca |*
*caraṇ'āśraya dānena kṛpāmayi namo'stu te ||*

Bestow Thy grace, O great Divinity, on us, Thy children bowing in prostration before Thee!
And grant us shelter at Thy feet, O Compassionate One! To Thee our salutations!

*5*

लज्जापटावृते नित्यं सारदे ज्ञानदायिके ।
पापेभ्यो नः सदा रक्ष कृपामयि नमोऽस्तुते ॥ ५ ॥

*Lajjā-paṭ'āvṛte nityaṁ Sārade jñāna-dāyike |*
*pāpebhyo naḥ sadā rakṣa kṛpā-mayi namo'stu te.*

Though ever covered with the veil of modesty, Thou, O Mother Sārada,
Art really the Power that bestows spiritual illumination on men.
Protect us from sins evermore, O Grace embodied! To Thee our salutations!

6

रामकृष्णगतप्राणां तन्नाम श्रवणप्रियाम् ।
तद् भावरञ्जिताकारां प्रणमामि मुहुर्मुहुः ॥ ६ ॥

*Rāmakṛṣṇa-gata-prāṇāṁ tan-nāma śravaṇa-priyām |*
*tad-bhāva-rañjit'ā kārāṁ praṇamāmi muhur-muhuḥ ||*

To Her whose life is fused into one with Rāmakṛṣṇa's,
Whose delight consists in absorption in thoughts and talks about His glories,
Whose personality is soaked and suffused with His spirit,
To Her my repeated salutations!

7

पवित्रं चरितं यस्याः पवित्रं जीवनं तथा ।
पवित्रतास्वरूपिण्यै तस्यै कुर्मो नमो नमः ॥ ७ ॥

*Pavitraṁ caritam yasyāḥ pavitraṁ jīvanam tathā |*
*pavitratā-svarūpiṇyai tasyai kurmo namo namaḥ ||*

To Her whose life-story is sanctifying,
To Her whose life breathes sanctity,
To Her who is verily sanctity embodied —
To Her our repeated salutations!

8

देवीं प्रसन्नां प्रणतार्तिहन्त्रीं योगीन्द्रपूज्यां युगधर्मपात्रीम् ।
तां सारदां भक्तिविज्ञानदात्रीं दयास्वरूपां प्रणमामि नित्यम् ॥ ८ ॥

*Devīṁ prasannāṁ praṇatārti-hantrīm*
*yogīndra-pūjyām yuga-dharma pātrīm* |
*tāṁ Śāradāṁ bhakti-vijñāna-dātrīm*
*dayā-svarūpāṁ praṇamāmi nityam* ||

My perpetual salutation to the gracious Mother Sārada, the embodiment of mercy and the granter of Bhakti and Jñāna —
To Her who (with Rāmakṛṣṇa) has given a new revelation for the present age,
And who assuages the miseries of devotees taking refuge at Her feet!

*9*

स्नेहेन बध्नासि मनोऽस्मदीयं
दोषानशेषान् सगुणीकरोषि ।
अहेतुना नो दयसे सदोषान्
स्वाङ्के गृहीत्वा यदिदं विचित्रम् ॥९ ॥

*Snehena badhnāsi mano'smadīyam*
*doṣān aśeṣān saguṇī karoṣi* |
*ahetunā no dayase sadoṣān*
*svāṅke gṛhītvā yad idam vicitram* ||

Binding our mind to Thee with the bonds of Thy love, Thou dost transmute our very vices into virtues.
Compassionate as Thou art without any consideration of merit,
Thou dost, lo! take even unworthy ones into Thy lap!

*10*

प्रसीद मातर्विनयेन याचे
नित्यं भव स्नेहवती सुतेषु ।
प्रेमैकबिन्दुं चिरदग्धचित्ते
विषिञ्च चित्तं कुरु नः सुशान्तम् ॥ १० ॥

*Prasīda mātar vinayena yāce*
*nityam bhava snehavatī suteṣu* |
*prem'aika-binduṁ cira-dagdha-citte*
*viṣiñca cittaṁ kuru naḥ suśāntam* ||

Mother, be propitious and grant what I in humility beseech!
May Thou be ever affectionate to us, Thy children!
And casting even a drop of Thy love on our long-parched heart,
Render it cool and peaceful!

11

जननीं सारदां देवीं रांमकृष्णं जगद्गुरुं ।
पादपद्मे तयोः श्रित्वा प्रणमामि मुहुर्मुहुः ॥ ११ ॥

*Jananīṁ Sāradāṁ devīṁ Rāmakṛṣṇaṁ jagad-gurum* |
*pāda-padme tayoḥ śritvā praṇamāmi muhur-muhuḥ* ||

Taking shelter at the feet of Sārada, the universal Mother,
And Rāmakṛṣṇa the Teacher of the world, I salute them again and again!

# ŚRĪ SĀRADĀDEVĪ DHYĀNAM

By Swāmi Abhedānanda

*1*

ध्यायेद्हृत्कमलमध्ये हेमवर्णां सुखासनाम् ।
आलुलायित केशार्ध वक्षस्थलाभिमण्डिताम् ॥

*Dhyāyet hṛt-kamala-madhye hema-varṇāṁ sukh'āsanām |*
*ālulāyita-keśārdha-vakṣa-sthal'ābhimaṇḍitām ||*

*2*

श्वेतवस्त्रावृतार्धाङ्गं हेमालङ्कार भूषिताम् ।
स्वक्रोडन्यस्त हस्ताञ्च द्विभुजां स्थिरलोचनाम् ॥

*Śveta-vastrā-vṛt'ārdh'āṅgāṁ hem'ālaṅkāra-bhūṣitām |*
*svakroḍa-nyasta-hastāñ ca dvibhujāṁ sthira-locanām ||*

*3*

प्रसन्नवदनां जीवदुःखगलितचेतसाम् ।
शुभ्रज्योतिर्मयीं देवीं वरदां सर्वमङ्गलाम् ॥

*Prasanna-vadanāṁ jīva-duḥkha-galita-cetasām |*
*śubhra-jyotirmayīṁ devīṁ varadāṁ sarva-maṅgalām ||*

*4*

रामकृष्णगतप्राणां तन्नामश्रवणप्रियाम् ।
तद्भावरञ्जिताकारां विश्वमातृस्वरूपिणीम् ॥

*Rāmakṛṣṇa-gata-prāṇāṁ tan-nāma-śravaṇa-priyām |*
*tad-bhāva-rañjit ākārāṁ viśva-mātṛ-svarūpiṇīm ||*

*5*

स्नेहमयीं शिवां शान्तां भक्तिमुक्तिप्रदायिनीम् ।
सर्वजीवत्राणकर्त्रीं सारदां ज्ञानदायिनीम् ॥

***Sneha-mayīṁ śivām śāntāṁ bhakti-mukti-***
*pradāyinīm |*
*sarva-jīva-trāṇa-kartrīṁ Sāradāṁ jñāna-dāyinīm.*

Let us meditate in the lotus of the heart on Mother Sārada —
Of golden hue;
Seated cross-legged;
Half of her dishevelled hair flowing down the chest;
Wrapped in white cloth;
Wearing golden bracelets;
With two palms crossed and resting in the lap;
Of steady gaze;
With visage beaming with grace;

And heart melting at the sorrows of living beings;
Radiant light of purity;
The bounteous;
Come for the good of all;
With life centered in Rāmakṛṣṇa and mind
ever delighting in his thought;
Veritably an embodiment of his ideas;
Manifestation of Universal Motherhood;
Overflowing with Universal benevolence,
goodness and peace;
Bestower of devotion and salvation;
Redeemer of all Jivas;
And giver of Divine Knowledge.

## SĀRADĀ-NĀMA SAṄKĪRTANAM

### By Swāmi Guṇātītānanda

*Meditation*

*1*

ध्यायेद्हृदम्बुजे देवीं तरुणारुणविग्रहाम् ।
वराभयकरां शान्तां स्मितोत्फुल्लमुखाम्बुजाम् ॥

*Dhyāyet-hṛdambuje devīṁ taruṇāruṇa-vigrahām*
*varābhaya-karāṁ śāntāṁ smit'otphulla-mukhāmbujām*

I meditate in the lotus of my heart on the Divine Mother whose form has the brilliance of the rising sun, whose hands are held in the pose of giving protection and boons, whose form is an embodiment of Peace, and whose smiling face is like a blooming lotus;

*2*

स्थलपद्म-प्रतीकाश-पादाम्भोज-सुशोभनाम् ।
शुक्लाम्बर-धरां धीरां लज्जापट-विभूषिताम् ॥

*Sthala-padma-pratīkāśa-pādāmbhoja-suśobhanām |*
*śuklāṁbara-dharāṁ dhīrām lajjāpaṭa-vibhuṣitām ||*

Whose feet have the splendour of a brilliant land lotus; who is dressed in a pure white cloth, who is a tower of spiritual Power, who is decorated by the veil of modesty;

*3*

प्रसन्नां धर्मकामार्थ-मोक्षदां विश्वमङ्गलाम् ।
स्वनाथ-वामभागस्थां भक्तानुग्रहकारिणीम् ॥

*Prasannāṁ dharma-kāmārtha-mokṣadām viśva-maṅgalām |*
*Svanātha-vāma-bhāgasthāṁ bhakt'ānugraha-kāriṇīm ||*

Who is a centre emitting Peace and Joy, who bestows on votaries moral excellence, desired objects, and liberation, who has come for the good of the world; who has appropriated the left half of Her Lord, and who is the source of blessings to devotees.

ॐ सर्वदेवदेवीस्वरूपिण्यै श्री· सारदादेव्यै नमः ।

*Om sarva-deva-devī-svarupiṇyai*
*śrī Sāradā devyai namaḥ*

Om, salutations to Srī Sāradā Devi who is the embodiment of all Devas and Devis!

त्वं मे ब्रह्मसनातनि मा ।
सारदयीश्वरी सुभगे मा ॥ त्वं मे.

*Tvam me brahma-sanātani mā*
*Sāradayīśvarī subhage mā Tvam me*

Thou art my Brahman Eternal., O Mother!
Heart-enchanting Divine Mother Sāradā.... Thou art my Brahman eternal!

1 ब्रह्मानन्द स्वरूपिणि मा ।

*Brahmānanda-svarūpiṇi mā*

O Mother, Thou who art of the nature of Brahmic Bliss!

2 ब्रह्मशक्ति सुख-दायिनि मा ।

*Brahma-śakti-sukha-dāyini mā*

O Mother, Thou the Power of Brahman and bestower of happiness!

3 सच्चित्सुखमय-रूपिणि मा ।

*Sac-cit-sukha-maya-rūpiṇi* *mā*

O Mother, Thou who art of the nature of Existence, Consciousness, and bliss!

4 सृष्टि-स्थिति-लय-कारिणि मा ।

*Sṛṣṭi-sthiti-laya-kāriṇi* *mā*

O Mother, Thou who the art cause of creation, sustentation and dissolution!

5 ब्रह्म सुधाम्बुधि-केलिनि मा ।

***Brahma-sudhāmbudhi-kelini*** *mā*

O Mother, Thou who sportest in the nectar of Brāhmic Bliss!

6 ब्रह्मात्मैक्य-शुभङ्करि मा ।

*Brahm'ātmaikya-śubhaṅkari* *mā*

O Mother, Thou who grantest the blessing of union of Ātma with Brahman!

7 जीवेश्वरभित्कौतुकि मा ।

*Jīv'eśvarabhit-kautuki* *mā*

O Mother, Thou who sportest by generating difference between the Jīva and Īśwara!

8 अगाधलीला-रूपिणि मा ।

*Agādha-līlā-rūpiṇi* *mā*

O Mother, Thou the meaning of whose sport is too deep to understand!

9 चिन्मयरूप-विलासिनि मा ।

*Cinmaya-rūpa-vilāsini* *mā*

O Mother, Thou who sportest with a form of Spiritual Essence!

10 बहिरन्तर-सुखवर्धिनि मा ।

*Bahi-rantara-sukha-vardhini* *mā*

O Mother, Thou who enhancest happiness within and without!

11 ज्ञानानन्द-प्रवर्षिणि मा ।

*Jñānānanda-pravarṣiṇi* *mā*

O Mother, Thou who inundates the aspirant with the Bliss of Consciousness!

12 दिव्यरसामृत-वर्षिणि मा ।

*Divya-rasāmṛta-varṣiṇi* *mā*

O Mother, Thou who rainest the nectar of Divine Essence!

13 मूलाधार-निवासिनि मा ।

*Mūlādhāra-nivāsini* *mā*

O Mother, Thou who residest in the Mūlādhāra!

14 सहस्रार-शिव-सङ्गिनि मा ।

*Sahasrāra-Śiva-saṅgini* *mā*

O Mother, Thou who art united with Śiva in the Sahasrāra!

15 आद्ये शक्ति-स्वरूपिणि मा ।

*Ādye śakti-svarūpiṇi* *mā*

O Mother, Thou who art the Original Universal Power!

16 चितिसुख-दायिनि-तारिणि मा ।

*Citi-sukha-dāyini-tāriṇi* *mā*

O Mother, Thou who bestowest spiritual bliss and savest aspirants!

17 शुभमति-दायिनि-शाङ्करि मा ।

*Śubha-mati-dāyiṇi-śāṅkari* *mā*

O Mother, Thou who art the Consort of Śiva and bestowest noble tendencies on the mind!

18 दुर्गति-दुर्मति-नाशिनि मा ।

*Durgati-durmati-nāśini* *mā*

O Mother, Thou who art the effacer of evil tendencies and thus the saviour of aspirants from downfall!

19 महाकाल-हृदि-नर्तिनि मा ।

*Mahākāla-hṛdi-nartini* *mā*

O Mother, Thou who dancest in the heart of Mahākāla!

20 जीवशिवान्तर-वर्तिनि मा ।

*Jīva-śivāntara-vartini* *mā*

O Mother, Thou who standest between Śiva and Jīva!

21 जगज्जननि जयदायिनि मा ।

*Jagaj-janani jaya-dāyini* *mā*

O Mother, Thou who hast given birth to the universe and who bestowest success on all enterprises!

22 तडिल्लसित-सौदामिनि मा ।

*Taḍil-lasita-saudāmini* *mā*

O Mother, Thou who resemblest the flash of lightning in a rain-cloud!

23 सीता-रामाकारिणि मा ।

*Sītā-Rām'ākāriṇi* *mā*

O Mother, Thou who art the Original Being that manifested as Sītā and Rāma!

24 कृष्ण-राधिका-रूपिणि मा ।

*Kṛṣṇa-rādhikā-rūpiṇi* *mā*

O Mother, Thou who assumest the forms of Kṛṣṇa and Rādhā!

25 कमनीयाकृति-धारिणि मा ।

*Kamanīyākṛti-dhāriṇi* *mā*

O Mother, Thou who art of enchanting form!

26 भवसागर-भय-हारिणि मा ।

*Bhava-sāgara-bhaya-hāriṇi* *mā*

O Mother, Thou who savest one from the fear of transmigratory existence!

27 शान्ति-सौख्य-चिर-दायिनि मा ।

*Śānti-saukhya-cira-dāyini* *mā*

O Mother, Thou who grantest the bliss of eternal Peace!

28 क्षान्ति-महागुण-वर्षिणि मा ।

*Kṣānti-mahāguṇa-varṣini* *mā*

O Mother, Thou who rainest the great virtue of patience!

29 कान्ति-वराभय-दायिनि मा ।

*Kānti-varābhaya-dāyini* *mā*

O Mother, Thou who bestowest splendour, boons and freedom from fear!

30 गिरिशाङ्कोपरि-वासिनी मा ।

*Giriś'āṅkopari-vāsini* *mā*

O Mother, Thou who art seated on the lap of Śiva, the Lord of Mountains!

31 हरार्ध-नारी-रूपिणि मा ।

*Harārdha-nārī-rūpiṇi* *mā*

O Mother, Thou who hast converted one half of Śiva's form into that of a woman who is Thyself!

32 नटन-महेश्वर-सङ्गिनि मा ।

*Naṭana-maheśvara-saṅgini* *mā*

O Mother, Thou who art the partner of Śiva and His Cosmic Dance!

33 हर-हर्षोत्करि-नर्तिनि मा ।

*Hara-harṣ'otkari-nartini* *mā*

O Mother, Thou who enhancest the joy of Śiva by Thy dance!

34 सारदेश्वरि-षोडशि मा ।

*Sāradeśvarī-ṣoḍaśi* *mā*

O Mother, Thou Sāradā who art none other than Ṣoḍaśi!

35 साधक-मानस-शोधिनि मा ।

*Sādhaka-mānasa-śodhini* *mā*

O Mother, Thou who enlightenest the mind of spiritual aspirants!

36 सर्व-सुभाग्य-प्रसादिनि मा ।

*Sarva-subhāgya-prasādini* *mā*

O Mother, Thou who bringest good fortune to one in all matters!

37 गुह-गजमुख-जनि-दायिनि मा ।

*Guha-gajamukha-jani-dāyini* *mā*

O Mother, Thou who gave birth to Guha (Subrahmaṇya) and Gaja-mukha (Gaṇapati)!

38 एकानेक-विभागिनि मा ।

*Ekāneka-vibhāgini* *mā*

O Mother, Thou who hast brought about the division of the One into the many!

39 हिमगिरि-नन्दिनि-लासिनि मा ।

*Himagiri-nandini-lāsini* *mā*

O Mother, Thou the playful Daughter of the Snow-clad Mountain!

40 सर्व-चराचर-सर्जिनि मा ।

*Sarva-carācara-sarjini* *mā*

O Mother, Thou who hast brought out all that moves and moves not !

41 सर्व-भवामय-वारिणि मा ।

*Sarva-bhavāmaya-vāriṇi* *mā*

O Mother, Thou who art the remedy for all the ills of Samsāra!

42 सर्व-जगत्रय-साक्षिणि मा ।

*Sarva-jagatraya-sākṣiṇi* *mā*

O Mother, Thou who art the witness of the three worlds!

43 निखिलाधीश्वरि योगिनि मा ।

*Nikhil'ādhīśvari yogini* *mā*

O Mother, Thou the Divine Female who is the mistress of all the worlds!

44 एला-गन्ध-सुकेशिनि मा ।

*Elā-gandha-sukeśini* *mā*

O Mother, Thou whose locks have the fragrance of Ela!

45 चिन्मय-सुन्दर-रूपिणि मा ।

*Cinmaya-sundara-rūpiṇi* *mā*

O Mother, Thou who hast a form of beauty that is purely spiritual!

46 परमानन्द-तरङ्गिणि मा ।

*Paramānanda-taraṅgiṇi* *mā*

O Mother, Thou in whom the waves of bliss are rolling!

47 रम्य-कान्ति-चिर-धारिणि मा ।

*Ramya-kānti-cira-dhāriṇi* *mā*

O Mother, Thou in whom resides inexhaustible spiritual splendour!

48 समस्त-सुगुणाभूषणि मा ।

*Samasta-suguṇ'ābhūṣaṇi* *mā*

O Mother, Thou who art decorated with the ornaments of all virtues!

49 सद्गति-सन्मति-दायिनि मा ।

*Sadgati-sanmati-dāyini* *mā*

O Mother, Thou who givest the Exalted Destiny and a mind with noble inclinations!

50 भवतारिणि-करुणेश्वरि मा ।

*Bhavatāriṇi-karuṇeśvari* *mā*

O Mother, Thou who art the goddess endowed with grace and the redeemer of man from Samsāra!

51 त्रिपुरे-सुन्दरि-मोहिनि मा ।

*Tripure sundari-mohini* *mā*

O Mother, Thou enchantress, who art known as Tripura-sundarī!

52 ब्रह्माण्डोदर-धारिणि मा ।

*Brahmāṇḍodara-dhāriṇi* *mā*

O Mother, Thou whose abdomen is the residence of the whole universe!

53 प्रेमानन्द-प्रवर्षिणि मा ।

*Premānanda-pravarṣiṇi* *mā*

O Mother, Thou who rainest the bliss of love!

54 सर्व-चराचर-पालिनि मा ।

*Sarva-carācara-pālini* *mā*

O Mother, Thou who art the protector of all that is moving and unmoving!

55 भुवन-चतुर्दश-प्रसविणि मा ।

*Bhuvana-caturdaśa-prasaviṇi* *mā*

O Mother, Thou who gave birth to all the fourteen spheres!

56 नाना-लीला-कारिणि मा ।

*Nānā-līlā-kāriṇi* *mā*

O Mother, Thou who art the cause of Divine Play in various forms!

57 विविध-विभूति-विधारिणि मा ।

*Vividha-vibhūti-vidhāriṇi* *mā*

O Mother, Thou who art endowed with Divine Powers of various kinds!

58 ज्ञानालोक-प्रदायिनि मा ।

*Jñānāloka-pradāyini* *mā*

O Mother, Thou who bestowest the insight of spiritual illumination!

59 विश्व-क्रीडा-कौतुकि मा ।

*Viśva-krīḍā-kautuki* *mā*

O Mother, Thou whose play consists in the creation, sustentation and dissolution of the whole universe!

60 विश्वाधिष्ठित चिन्मयि मा ।

*Viśv'ādhiṣṭhita cinmayi* *mā*

O Mother, Thou who art the Basic Substance forming the support of the whole changing universe!

61 मन्दस्मित स्मरहारिणि मा ।

*Manda-smita smara-hāriṇi* *mā*

O Mother, Thou who stole the heart of Hara (Śiva) by Thy smile!

62 भक्तानुग्रह-कारिणि मा ।

*Bhakt'ānugraha-kāriṇi* *mā*

O Mother, Thou who blessest the devotees!

63 योग-भोग-वर-दायिनि मा ।

*Yoga-bhoga-vara-dāyini* *mā*

O Mother, Thou who bestowest the boon of enjoyment and spiritual inclination!

64 शान्ति-सुधा-निस्स्यन्दिनि मा ।

*Śānti-sudhā-nissyandini* *mā*

O Mother, Thou from whom the nectar of Peace is ever flowing!

65 भ्रान्ति-रोगविष-हारिणि मा ।

*Bhrānti-roga-viṣa-hāriṇi* *mā*

O Mother, Thou who curest the disease born of the poison of illusory phenomenal perception!

66 कान्ति-योग-सुख-दायिनि मा ।

*Kānti-yoga-sukha-dāyini* *mā*

O Mother, Thou who grantest happiness, splendour and spirituality!

67 वीर-नरेन्द्र-प्रहर्षिणि मा ।

*Vīrā-Narendra-praharṣiṇi* *mā*

O Mother, Thou who gladdened the heart of heroic Narendra!

68 समाधि-चिर-चिति-दायिनि मा ।

*Samādhi-cira-citi-dāyini* *mā*

O Mother, Thou who grantest permanent steadiness of mind in the Supreme Spirit!

69 वीर्य-बलाभय-कारिणि मा ।

*Vīrya-bal'ābhaya-kāriṇi* *mā*

O Mother, Thou who art the cause of heroism, strength and fearlessness!

70 तापत्रयभय-हारिणि मा ।

*Tāpa-traya-bhaya-hāriṇi* *mā*

O Mother, Thou who remediest the threefold misery and all fears!

71 सर्वोत्तुङ्ग-सुवासिनि मा ।

*Sarvottuṅga-suvāsini* *mā*

O Mother, Thou who art the Highest Being dwelling in all that exists!

72 प्रसन्न-वरदे-भैरवि मा ।

*Prasanna-varade-bhairavi* *mā*

O Mother, Thou art beneficent and boon-giving though the fear-generating, Bhairavi!

73 हवन-जपार्चन-साधिनि मा ।

*Havana-japārcana-sādhini* *mā*

O Mother, Thou generator in one of the desire to do fire-sacrifice, Japa and flower offerings!

74 चण्डासुर-खल-घातिनि मा ।

*Caṇḍāsura-khala-ghātini* *mā*

O Mother, Thou who destroyed the brutal Asura Caṇḍa!

75 सकल-देव-जय-साधिनि मा ।

*Sakala-deva-jaya-sādhini* *mā*

O Mother, Thou who enablest aspirants to transcend the status of all Devas!

76 दुष्ट-मुण्ड-वधकारिणि मा ।

*Duṣṭa-muṇḍa-vadha-kāriṇi* *mā*

O Mother, Thou who slew the cruel demon Muṇḍa!

77 चामुण्डेश्वरी दर्पिणि मा ।

*Cāmuṇḍ'eśvari darpiṇi* *mā*

O Mother, Thou who art famous as the Godness Cāmuṇḍā!

78 माहिष-दर्प-विनाशिनि मा ।

*Māhiṣa-darpa-vināśini* *mā*

O Mother, Thou who humbled the pride of Mahiṣāsura!

79 माहेश्वर-सुख-वर्धिनि मा ।

*Māheśvara-sukha-vardhini* *mā*

O Mother, Thou who enhancest the joy of Maheśvara (Śiva)!

80 महिषासुर-खल-मर्दिनि मा ।

*Mahiṣāsura-khala-mardini* *mā*

O Mother, Thou who destroyed the evil Asura known as Mahiṣa!

81 त्रिगुण-त्रिलोक-त्रिरूपिणि मा ।

*Triguṇa-triloka-trirūpiṇi* *mā*

O Mother, Thou who art the three Guṇās, the three worlds and art of three forms!

82 निर्गुण-सगुण-विचित्रिणि मा ।

*Nirguṇa-saguṇa-vicitriṇi* *mā*

O Mother, Thou who art unique as being both with attributes and without attributes!

83 कारित-ध्यानानन्दिनि मा ।

*Kārita-dhyān'ānandini* *mā*

O Mother, Thou who bestowest the blissful state of meditation!

84 दर्पण-चित्त-विभासिनि मा ।

*Darpaṇa-citta-vibhāsini* *mā*

O Mother, Thou who reflectest Thyself in the mirror of the mind!

85 चेतो-दर्पण-काशिनि मा ।

*Ceto-darpaṇa-kāśini* *mā*

O Mother, Thou who purifiest the mirror of the mind!

86 नव-नव-रूप-सुदर्शिनि मा ।

*Nava-nava-rūpa-sudarśani* *mā*

O Mother, Thou who revealest Thyself in ever-novel forms!

87 समस्त-लोकोद्धारिणि मा ।

*Samasta-lokoddhāriṇi* *mā*

O Mother, Thou who art the redeemer of the whole world!

88 रामकृष्ण-नवरूपिणि मा ।

*Rāmakṛṣṇa-nava rūpiṇi* *mā*

O Mother, Thou who art only a newly assumed form of Rāmakṛṣṇa!

89 धर्मग्लानि-विनाशिनि मा ।

*Dharma-glāni-vināśini* *mā*

O Mother, Thou who checked the decadence of Dharma!

90 धर्मस्थापन-कारिणि मा ।

*Dharma-sthāpana-kāriṇi* *mā*

O Mother, Thou who caused the establishment of Dharma!

91 रम्य-सहज-पथ-दर्शिनि मा ।

*Ramya-sahaja-patha-darśini* *mā*

O Mother, Thou who hast revealed the delightful path of Sahaja!

92 मातृभाव-सुख-शोधिनि मा ।

*Mātṛbhāva-sukha-śodhini* *mā*

O Mother, Thou who revealed the excellence of motherly attitude!

93 निर्मलभक्तोत्कर्षिणि मा ।

*Nirmala-bhakt'otkarṣiṇi* *mā*

O Mother, Thou who upliftest pure-minded devotees!

94 दिव्याद्भुत-चरितार्थिनि मा ।

*Divy'ādbhuta-caritārthini* *mā*

O Mother, Thou whose life is significant by its astonishing Divine excellences!

95 रामकृष्ण-सहधर्मिणि मा ।

*Rāmakṛṣṇa-sahadharmiṇi* *mā*

O Mother, Thou who art Rāmakṛṣṇa's companion in pursuing the ideal of Dharma!

*Jayarāmākhya-suvāṭini* *mā*

O Mother, Thou who took Thy birth in Jayrām-bāti!

97 मृग-केसरिवर-वाहिनि मा ।

*Mṛga-kesari-vara-vāhini* *mā*

O Mother, Thou who hast the Lion, the King of Beasts, as Thy mount!

98 दुर्ग-हिमाचल-नन्दिनि मा ।

*Durga-himācala-nandini* *mā*

O Mother, Thou who art the daughter of the Mountain of Snow, which is difficult of access!

99 नरेन्द्र-हृदय-निवासिनि मा ।

*Narendra-hṛdaya-nivāsini* *mā*

O Mother, Thou who residest in the heart of Narendra!

100 लोकोत्तरकृति-दर्शिनि मा ।

*Lokottara-kṛti-darśini* *mā*

O Mother, Thou who revealed in Thy life, excellences that are never seen in the world!

101 सुन्दररूप-विकाशिनि मा ।

*Sundara-rūpa-vikāśini* *mā*

O Mother, Thou who bore an enchanting form!

102 दिव्यगुणाकर-धारिणि मा ।

*Divya-guṇākara-dhāriṇi* *mā*

O Mother, Thou who art an embodiment of Divine excellences!

103 दुर्बल-सबल-सुकारिणि मा ।

*Durbala-sabala-sukāriṇi* *mā*

O Mother, Thou who art the cause of both strength and weakness!

104 दुःख-दैन्य-भय-नाशिनि मा ।

*Duḥkha-dainya-bhaya-nāśini* *mā*

O Mother, Thou who destroyest sorrow, suffering and fear!

105 सर्वभूतहित-साधिनि मा ।

*Sarva-bhūtahita-sādhini* *mā*

O Mother, Thou who accomplishest the good of all beings!

106 समस्त-लोकाभयकरि मा ।

*Samasta-lok'ābhayakari* *mā*

O Mother, Thou who givest shelter from fear to all beings!

107 दुर्गति-नाशिनि-दुर्गे मा ।

*Durgati-nāśini Durge* *mā*

O Mother, Thou goddess Durga who does arrest one's spiritual degradation!

108 नारायणि-जगदाद्ये मा ।
जय जय जय जगदाद्ये मा ।
नारायणि जय दुर्गे मा ।

*Nārayaṇi-jagad-ādye* *mā*
*Jaya jaya jaya jagad'ādye* *mā*
*Nārāyaṇi jaya Durge* *mā*

O Mother, Thou Nārāyaṇī, the Origin of all the worlds! Hail, Hail, Hail unto Thee, the Original Being!
O Mother, Thou Nārāyaṇī, the Origin of all the worlds.

## IN PRAISE OF THE MOTHER

अनन्तरूपिणि अनन्तगुणवति अनन्त-नाम्नि गिरिजे मा ।
शिवहृन्मोहिनि विश्वविलासिनि रामकृष्णजय-दायिनि मा ।।

*Anantarūpiṇi anantaguṇavati*
*ananta-nāmni girije* *mā* |
*Śivahṛnmohini viśvavilāsini*
*Rāmakṛṣṇa jaya - dāyini* *mā*||

O Mother, Thou Girijā with endless forms, endless excellences and endless names!
O Mother, Thou who enchantest the heart of Śiva, sportest as the worlds, and makest the life of Rāmakṛṣṇa meaningful.

2

जगज्जननि त्रिलोकपालिनि विश्वसुवासिनि शुभदे मा ।
दुर्गतिनाशिनि सन्मतिदायिनि भोग-मोक्षसुख-कारिणि मा ।।

*Jagajjanani trilokapālini*
*viśva-suvāsini śubhade* *mā* |
*durgatināśini sanmatidāyini*
*bhoga - mokṣasukha - kāriṇi* *mā* ||

O Mother, Thou the origin of the three worlds, the protector of the three worlds, the resident of all the worlds, and the grantor of all that is good!
O Mother, Thou the destroyer of evil destiny, the bestower of good tendencies and the cause of both worldly welfare and liberation.

परमे पार्वति सुन्दरि भगवत्ति दुर्गे भामति त्वं मे मा ।
प्रसीद मातर्नगेन्द्र-नन्दिनि चिरसुखदायिनि जयदे मा ।।

*Parame Pārvati sundari bhagavati*
*Durge bhāmati tvam me* *mā* |

*prasīda mātar nagendra- nandini*
*cira-sukha dāyini jaya de mā* ||

O Mother mine, Thou Pārvati, the Supreme Durgā, the Graceful, Possessor of all Powers, and the Illuminator of the Mind!

O Mother, be gracious, Thou the daughter of the mountain, the bestower of long-standing happiness and victory everywhere!

# STOTRA-RATNA
## By Śrī Yāmunācārya

[The twenty nine verses included in this Book of Hymns are selections from the great hymn, *Stotra-ratna* of Srī Yāmunācārya, one of the great preceptors of the Śrī-Vaiṣṇava sect. The excellence of the composition as a hymn in praise of God has won for it this name, meaning a jewel among hymns.

The Supreme Being is looked upon by the Srī-Vaiṣṇavas as Viṣṇu, referred to by His most sacred name Nārāyaṇa, meaning He who is the support and resting place of Jīvas (Nāras). Srī-Vaiṣṇavism teaches that God is the Antaryāmin (Indweller), and the Jīvas and the worlds form His adjuncts or limbs. He is the soul of the universe in a cosmic sense, and He is also the soul of every Jīva and every atom in the universe. Man exists for His sake as a limb on the body exists for an organism. Forgetful of this the Jīva lives an individuality-centred life—a life in which he conceives himself to be the centre for which everything else exists. The purpose of Vaiṣṇava religion is to shake man from this self-centred life and make Him feel that himself and the whole universe are God-centred and exist out of His will for His service. To feel thus that one is the property of the Supreme and to live in entire submission to Him is the goal to be achieved in life. The hymn given below is an expression of this devotional sentiment.

The whole hymn consists of sixty-five verses. From this we have selected the following twenty-nine verses which form the core of the hymn without any theological predilection, and can therefore be appreciated by any devotee, to whatever religion he might belong. The excluded verses are mainly the description of the form and attributes of Viṣṇu. What we have selected are verses of the nature of prayer, adoration, and self-surrender.]

1

नमो नमो वाङ्मनसाति-भूमये नमो नमो वाङ्मनसैकभूमये ।
नमो नमोऽनन्तमहाविभूतये नमो नमोऽनन्तदयैकसिन्धवे ॥

*Namo namo vāṅ-manas'āti bhūmaye*
*namo namo vāṅ-manas'aika bhūmaye* |
*namo namo'nanta -mahā-vibhūtaye*
*namo namo'nanta-day'aika-sindhave* ||

Hail, hail unto Thee who transcendest the ken of both speech and mind!
Hail, hail unto Thee who art the sole support of all that can be denoted by mind and speech!
Hail, hail unto Thee who art possessed of infinite Divine Powers!
Hail, hail unto Thee who art the one ocean of all that is known as grace!

*2*

न धर्मनिष्ठोऽस्मि न चात्मवेदी न भक्तिमांस्त्वच्चरणारविन्दे ।
अकिञ्चनोऽनन्यगतिश्शरण्य त्वत्पादमूलं शरणं प्रपद्ये ॥

*Na dharma-niṣṭho'smi na c'ātmavedī*
*na bhaktimāṁs tvatc-caraṇ'āravinde* |
*akiñcano' nanya-gatiś śaraṇya*
*tvad-pāda-mūlaṁ śaraṇaṁ prapadye* ||

Neither am I established in the practice of Dharma,
Nor in the knowledge that 'I am the Ātman (a spiritual monad)'!
I am not also endowed with devotion to Thy lotus feet.
O Bestower of Refuge! Destitute as I am of all virtues and powers, I have no shelter except Thee.

*3*

न निन्दितं कर्म तदस्ति लोके सहस्रशो यन्न मया व्यधायि ।
सोऽहं विपाकावसरे मुकुन्द क्रन्दामि सम्प्रत्यगतिस्तवाग्रे ॥

*Na ninditaṁ karma tadasti loke*
*sahasraśo yan na mayā vyadhāyi* |
*so'haṁ vipāk'āvasare Mukunda*
*krandāmi samprat'yagatis tavāgre* ||

There is no heinous act known in this world that I have not committed thousands of times, O Mukunda!
Now, when these acts are about to fructify into their evil consequences,
I wail in utter distress before Thee, having none else to redeem me from them.

*4*

निमज्जतोऽनन्त भवार्णवान्त - श्चिराय मे कूलमिवासि लब्धः ।
त्वयापि लब्धं भगवन्निदानी - मनुत्तमं पात्रमिदं दयायाः ॥

*Nimajjato'nanta bhav'ārṇavāntaś*
*cirāya me kūlam iv'āsi labdhaḥ* |
*tvay'āpi labdhaṁ bhagavann idānīm*
*anuttamaṁ pātram idam dayāyāḥ* ||

O Infinite Being! At last I, who have been sinking in the depths of this ocean of Samsāra, have found in Thee a shore of shelter;
And Thou, O Supreme Lord! hast now got in me the most fitting recipient for Thy grace.

*5*

अभूतपूर्वं मम भावि किं वा सर्वं सहे मे सहजं हि दुःखम् ।
किन्तु त्वदग्रे शरणागतानां पराभवो नाथ न तेऽनुरूपः ॥

*Abhūta-pūrvaṁ mama bhāvi kiṁ vā*
*sarvaṁ sahe me sahajaṁ hi duḥkham* |
*kintu tvad-agre śaraṇ'āgatānām* |
*parābhavo nātha na te'nurūpaḥ* ||

Is there anything worse to happen to me than what has already happened?
If so, I shall patiently bear them all, because misery has become something natural to me.
But, O Lord! Though it be so, downfall to one like me who has sought refuge in Thee is not befitting Thy honour and majesty.

*6*

निरासकस्यापि न तावदुत्सहे महेश हातुं तव पादपङ्कजम् ।
रुषा निरस्तोऽपि शिशुस्स्तनन्धयो न जातु मातुश्चरणौ जिहासति ॥

*Nirāsakasy'āpi na tāvad utsahe*
*maheśa hātuṁ tava pāda-paṅkajam*
*ruṣā nirasto'pi śiśu stan'andhayo*
*na jātu mātuś caraṇau jihāsati* ||

Even if Thou spurnest me, I cannot, O Lord of all, abandon my hold on Thy lotus feet,
Like an infant hungering for a feed at its mother breast does not move away from her, even if spurned by her in annoyance.

तवामृतस्यन्दिनि पादपङ्कजे निवेशितात्मा कथमन्यदिच्छति ।
स्थितेऽरविन्दे मकरन्दनिर्भरे मधुव्रतो नेक्षुरकं हि वीक्षते ॥

*Tav'āmṛta-syandini pāda-paṅkaje*
*niveśit'ātmā katham anyad icchati* |
*sthite'ravinde makaranda nirbhare*
*madhuvrato n'ekṣurakaṁ hi vīkṣate* ||

How can a mind that is steeped in the nectar-dripping lotus of Thy feet desire for anything else to enjoy?
A honey bee well-settled on a lotus flower full of honey
Never cares even to look at the flower Ikṣuraka with no fragrance or honey!

*8*

त्वदङ्घ्रिमुद्दिश्य कदापि केनचि - द्यथा तथा वापि सकृत्कृतोऽञ्जलिः ।
तदैव मुष्णात्यशुभान्यशेषत - श्शुभानि पुष्णाति न जातु हीयते ॥

*Tvad-aṅghrim- uddiśya kadāpi kenacid*
*yathā tathā vāpi sakṛt-kṛto' ñjaliḥ* |
*tad'aiva muṣṇāty aśubhāny aśeṣastaś-*
*śubhāni puṣṇāti na jātu hīyate* ||

Whoever, in whatever situation and in whatever manner adores Thee even once,

Even that redeems him from all sins, and works for his upliftment — it never goes in vain.

*9*

उदीर्णसंसारदवाशुशुक्षणिं क्षणेन निर्वाप्य परां च निर्वृतिम् ।
प्रयच्छति त्वच्चरणारुणाम्बुज - द्वयानुरागामृतसिन्धुशीकरः ॥

*Udīrṇa-saṁsāra-davāśu śukṣaṇim*
*kṣaṇena nirvāpya parāṁ ca nirvṛtim* |
*prayacchati tvac-caraṇ'āruṇ'āmbuja-*
*dvay'ānurāgāmṛta-sindhu-śīkaraḥ* ||

Even a particle of the ocean of love for Thy lotus feet
In no time extinguishes the flaming forest fire of Samsāra and bestows the Supreme Peace.

*10*

विलासविक्रान्तपरावरालयं नमस्यदार्तिक्षपणे कृतक्षणम् ।
धनं मदीयं तव पादपङ्कजं कदा नु साक्षात्करवाणि चक्षुषा ॥

*Vilāsa-vikrānta-parāvar'ālayam*
*namasyad-ārti-kṣapaṇe kṛtakṣaṇam* |
*dhanaṁ madīyaṁ tava pāda-paṅkajam*
*kadā nu sākṣāt-karavāṇi cakṣuṣā* ||

My wealth consists in Thy lotus feet which, O Trivikrama, measured all the worlds in three strides,

And which immediately redresses the miseries of those who prostrate before them.
When is it that I shall I directly experience them?

*11*

कदा पुनश्शङ्खरथाङ्गकल्पक - ध्वजारविन्दाङ्कुशवज्रलाञ्छनम् ।
त्रिविक्रम त्वच्चरणाम्बुजद्वयं मदीयमूर्धानमलङ्करिष्यति ॥

*Kadā punaś śaṅkha-rathāṅga-kalpaka-*
*dhvaj'āravind'āṅkuśa-vajra-lāñchanam* |
*Trivikrama tvac-caraṇ'āmbuja-dvayam*
*madīya-mūrdhānaṁ alaṅkariṣyati* ||

When again, O Trivikrama, will I be blessed with Thy feet placed on my head —
The feet that have the marking of conch, discus, the wish-yielding heavenly tree, flag, lotus, thunderbolt weapon and hook?

*12*

अचिन्त्यदिव्याद्भुतनित्ययौवन - स्वभावलावण्यमयामृतोदधिम् ।
श्रियः श्रियं भक्तजनैकजीवितं समर्थमापत्सखमर्थिकल्पकम् ॥

*Acintya-divy'ādbhuta-nitya-yauvana*
*svabhāva-lāvaṇya-may'āmṛt'o dadhim* |
*śriyaḥ śriyaṁ bhakta-janaika-jīvitam*
*samartham āpat-sakham arthi-kalpakam* ||

Thou who art the repository of inconceivable and never-fading youth and beauty;
Thou who art the abode of Śrī and the sustenance of devotees;
Thou who art the possessor of all powers;
Thou who art the friend in times of danger and the generous patron of devotees —

*13*

भवन्तमेवानुचरन्निरन्तरं प्रशान्तनिश्शेषमनोरथान्तरः ।
कदाहमैकान्तिकनित्यकिङ्करः प्रहर्षयिष्यामि सनाथजीवितः ॥

*Bhavantam ev'ānucaran nirantaram*
*praśānta-niśśeṣa manorath'āntaraḥ* |
*kad'āham'aikāntika-nitya-kiṅkaraḥ*
*praharṣayiṣyāmi sanātha-jīvitaḥ* ||

When shall I, having found my life's fulfilment
In being the eternal and whole-hearted servant of such a Master as Thee,
Rejoice by waiting on Thee always.

*14*

धिगशुचिमविनीतं निर्भयं मामलज्जं परमपुरुष योऽहं योगिवर्याग्रगण्यैः ।
विधिशिवसनकाद्यैर्ध्यातुमत्यन्तदूरं तव परिजनभावं कामये कामवृत्तः ॥

*Dhig aśucim avinītam nirbhayaṁ mām alajjam*
*parama-puruṣa yo'ham yogivary'āgragaṇyaiḥ* |

*Vidhi-Śiva-Sanakādyair dhyātum atyanta-dūram*
*tava parijana-bhāvaṁ kāmaye kāmavṛttaḥ* ||

Fie upon me — one who is a slave of desires,
Impure, impudent, cruel and immodest —
For aspiring to be a servant of Thee
Whom Brahmā and Śiva and great sages like Sanaka
Find it difficult even to conceive in their minds.

*15*

अपराधसहस्रभाजनं पतितं भीमभवार्णवोदरे ।
अगतिं शरणागतं हरे कृपया केवलमात्मसात्कुरु ॥

*Aparādha-sahasra-bhājanam*
*patitam bhīma-bhavārṇav'odare* |
*agatim śaraṇ'āgatam Hare*
*kṛpayā kevalam ātmasāt kuru*

Me who am guilty of innumerable sins,
Me who am drowning in the terrible ocean of Saṁsāra,
Me who, having none to support or sustain, have now taken full refuge in Thee —
Deign to take me, this worthless refugee, as Thy own out of Thy mercy alone.

16

अविवेकघनान्धदिङ्मुखे बहुधा सन्ततदुःखवर्षिणि ।
भगवन् भवदुर्दिने पथः स्खलितं मामवलोकयाच्युत ॥

*Aviveka-ghanāndha-diṅ-mukhe*
*bahudhā santata-duḥkha-varṣiṇi* |
*bhagavan bhava-durdine pathaḥ*
*skhalitaṁ mām avalokay'ācyuta* ||

O Lord who has no decay! Cast a sympathetic glance at me,
Who has slipped down on the path of life on this rainy day,
When the sky of my mind is overcast with the clouds of ignorance,
And the constant rain of miseries is continuing unceasingly.

*17*

न मृषा परमार्थमेव मे श्रृणु विज्ञापनमेकमग्रतः ।
यदि मे न दयिष्यसे ततो दयनीयस्तव नाथ दुर्लभः ॥

*Na mṛṣā paramārtham eva me*
*śṛṇu vijñāpanam ekam agrataḥ*|
*yadi me na dayiṣyase tato*
*dayanīyas tava nātha durlabhaḥ* ||

Hearken, O Lord, to this my only submission,
Which I make to Thee in truth, with no touch of pretension —
If Thou failest to feel pity for me,
Thou shalt not get another so deserving to be pitied.

*18*

तदहं त्वदृते न नाथवान् मदृते त्वं दयनीयवान्न च ।
विधिनिर्मितमेतमन्वयं भगवन् पालय मा स्म जीहपः ॥

*Tadaham tvad'ṛte na nāthavān*
*mad'ṛte tvam dayanīyavān na ca* |
*vidhi-nirmitam etam-anvayam*
*bhagavan pālaya mā sma jīhapaḥ* ||

Without Thee I shall be without a Master,
And without me Thou shalt not be considered compassionate.
Fate seems to have ordained this relationship between us. Please spurn me not.

*19*

वपुरादिषु योऽपि कोऽपि वा गुणतोऽसानि यथातथाविधः ।
तदयं तव पादपद्मयो - रहमद्यैव मया समर्पितः ॥

*Vapurādiṣu yo'pi ko'pi vā*
*guṇato'sāni yathā-tathā-vidhaḥ* |
*tadayaṁ tava pāda padmayor*
*aham ady'aiva mayā samarpitaḥ* |

Whatever type of body-mind I might get according to the play of Guṇas (dispositions of Nature),
The entity, denoted by the term 'I', is being offered at Thy lotus feet even now.

## *20*

मम नाथ यदस्ति योऽस्म्यहं सकलं तद्धि तवैव माधवं ।
नियतस्वमिति प्रबुद्धधी - रथवा किं नु समर्पयामि ते ॥

*Mama nātha yad asti yo'smyaham*
*sakalaṁ tadd hi tav'āiva mādhava* |
*niyata-svam iti prabuddha-dhīr*
*aṭhavā kiṁ nu samarpayāmi te* ||

My whole being' and whatever it possesses, all that, O Lord, are already Thine.
Being awakened to this eternally valid truth,
How, at all, can I *really* offer myself to Thee?

## *21*

अवबोधितवानिमां यथा मयि नित्यां भवदीयतां स्वयम् ।
कृपयैवमनन्यभोग्यतां भगवन् भक्तिमपि प्रयच्छ मे ॥

*Avabodhitavān imām yathā*
*mayi nityāṁ bhavadīyatāṁ svayam* |
*kṛpay'aivam ananya-bhogyatām*
*bhagavan bhaktim api prayaccha me* ||

Being thus enlightened by Thy grace
With the consciousness that I am naturally and eternally Thine,
Bestow on me out of Thy grace that type of devotion
Which makes me feel Thy service as my only concern.

22

तव दास्यसुखैकसङ्गिनां भवनेष्वस्त्वपि कीटजन्म मे ।
इतरावसथेषु मा स्म भू - दपि मे जन्म चतुर्मुखात्मना ॥

*Tava dāsya-sukh'aika-saṅginām*
*bhavaneṣv'astv'api kīṭa-janma me* |
*itarā-vasatheṣu mā sma bhūd*
*api me janma catur-mukh'ātmanā* ||

May I be reborn, even if it be as a worm,
Only in the houses of those whose sole delight is Thy service,
And may I not get embodiment in the houses of people who are otherwise disposed,
Be it even the four-faced Brahmā.

23

सकृ त्वदाकारविलोकनाशया तृणीकृतानुत्तमभुक्तिमुक्तिभिः ।
महात्मभिर्मामवलोक्यतां नय क्षणेऽपि ते यद्विरहोऽतिदुःसहः ॥

*Sakṛt tvad-ākāra-vilokan'āśayā*
*tṛṇīkṛtān uttama-bhukti-muktibhiḥ* |
*mahātmabhir mām avalokyatām naya*
*kṣaṇ'epi te yad viraho'ti-duḥsahaḥ*

Raise me to a state in which I will be noticed and befriended by great ones,

Who, prompted by the desire to get even a glimpse of Thee,
Have abandoned the coveted fulfilments of worldly enjoyments and liberation,
And whose separation even for a moment is unbearable to Thee.

*24*

न देहं न प्राणान्न च सुखमशेषाभिलषितं न चात्मानं नान्यत्किमपि तव शेषत्वविभवात् ।
बहिर्भूतं नाथ क्षणमपि सहे यातु शतधा विनाशं तत्सत्यं मधुमथन विज्ञापनमिदम् ॥

*Na deham na prāṇān na ca sukham aśeṣ'ābhilaṣitam*
*na c'ātmānam n'ānyat kim api tava śeṣatva-vibhavāt* |
*bahir-bhūtam nātha kṣaṇam api sahe yātu śatadhā*
*vināśam tat satyam madhu-mathana vijñāpanam idam* ||

O Lord, neither the body, nor the Prāṇa, nor the universally coveted happiness,
Nor the self, nor anything else besides these,
If they are not for Thy service, can be entertained by me even for a moment —
Let them be shattered into a hundred shreds. This, O Slayer of Madhu,
Is my true resolution, and this my submission before Thee.

25

दुरन्तस्यानादेरपरिहरणीयस्य महतो निहीनाचारोऽहं नृपशुरशुभस्यास्पदमपि ।
दयासिन्धो बन्धो निरवधिकवात्सल्यजलधे तव स्मारं स्मारं गुणगणमितीच्छामि
गतभीः ॥

*Durantasy'ānāder apariharaṇīyasya mahato*
*nihīn'ācāro'haṁ nṛ-paśur aśubhasy'āspadam api* |
*dayāsindho bandho niravadhika-vātsalya-jaladhe*
*tava smāraṁ smāraṁ guṇa-gaṇam it'īcchāmi*
*gatabhīḥ* |

Though I, a beast of a man, am the repository of sins
That are beginningless, remediless, and foreboding doom,
Still, O Ocean of Mercy, O Friend of all, O the Repository of inexhaustible Love!
I address this prayer of mine, remembering again and again Thy great attributes mentioned above.

26

अमर्यादः क्षुद्रश्चलमतिरसूयाप्रसवभूः कृतघ्नो दुर्मानी स्मरपरवशो वञ्चनपरः ।
नृशंसः पापिष्ठः कथमहमितो दुःखजलधे - रपारादुत्तीर्णस्तव
परिचरेयं चरणयोः ॥

*Amaryādaḥ kṣudraś calamatir asūyā-prasava-bhūḥ*
*kṛtaghno durmānī smara-paravaśo vañcana-paraḥ* |
***nṛ'śaṁsaḥ pāpiṣṭhaḥ katham aham ito duḥkha-jaladher***
*apārād uttīrṇas tava paricareyam caraṇayoḥ* ||

I have been a transgressor of good conduct,
Evil-minded, fickle-minded, jealous by nature, ungrateful,
And arrogant, deceitful, lascivious, cruel and sinful.
How can I get out of this shoreless ocean of misery
And become a servant at Thy Holy feet?

27

रघुवर यदभूस्त्वं तादृशो वायसस्य प्रणत इति दयालुर्यच्च चैद्यस्य कृष्ण ।
प्रतिभवमपराद्धुर्मुग्ध सायूज्यदोऽभू - र्वद किमपदमागस्तस्य
तेऽस्ति क्षमायाः ॥

*Raghuvara yadabhūs tvam tādṛśo vāyasasya*
*praṇata iti dayālur yac ca Caidyasya Kṛṣṇa* |
*pratibhavam aparāddhur mugdha-sāyūjyado'bhūr*
*vada kim apadam āgas tasya te'sti kṣamāyāḥ* ||

O Lord of Raghus! It is well known how Thou didst become gracious
To the wicked crow only because it bowed down at Thy feet.

And how Thou, forgiving all the sinful actions of the King of Cedi
Bestowed on him the most elevated state of oneness with Thee.
Say then what mistake is beyond the pale of Thy mercy.

*28*

अनिच्छन्नप्येवं यदि पुनरितीच्छन्निव रज - स्तमश्छन्नच्छद्मस्तुतिवचन भङ्गीमरचयम्
तथापीत्थं रूपं वचनमवलम्ब्यापि कृपया त्वमेवैवंभूतं धरणिधर मे शिक्षय मनः ॥

*Anicchann apy evam yadi punar itīcchann iva rajas-*
*tamaś-channacchadma-stuti-vacana-bhaṅgīm aracayam* |
*tath'āpī'ttham rūpaṁ vacanam avalambyā'pi kṛpayā*
*tvam ev aivam-bhūtam dharaṇi-dhara me śikṣaya manaḥ* |

Steeped as I am in Rajas and Tamas, I have approached Thee in an attitude of pretended devotion,
As if I truly desire for those great blessings as my fine words seem to convey.
Even if it be so, O Thou the Bearer of the whole burden of the world!
Do Thou educate my mind on these lines, accepting the letter of my prayer, hypocritical though it may be.

*29*

पिता त्वं माता त्वं दयिततनयस्त्वं प्रियसुहृ - त्त्वमेव त्वं मित्रं
गुरुरसि गतिश्चासि जगताम् ।
त्वदीयस्त्वद्भृत्यस्तव परिजनस्त्वद्गतिरहं प्रपन्नश्चैवं सत्यहमपि
तवैवास्मि हि भरः ॥

*Pitā tvam mātā tvam dayita-tanayas-tvam priya-suhṛt-*
*tvam eva tvaṁ mitraṁ gurur asi gatiś c'āsi jagatām |*
*tvadīyas tvad-bhṛtyas tava parijanas tvad-gatir aham*
*prapannaś c'aivam saty aham api tav'aivāsmi hi bharaḥ ||*

Being the Teacher and the Refuge of the whole world,
Thou art my father, mother, beloved son, dear comrade and loving friend.
I am Thy devotee, Thy servant, Thy attendant, and one having Thee as my sole support and goal.
I am a refugee at Thy feet and therefore my whole burden rests on Thee.

# GOPIKĀ-GĪTAM
## (From Śrīmad Bhāgavatam)

[ Gopikā-Gītam or the 'Hymn of the Gopikas' forms the 31st chapter of the 10th Skandha of Śrīmad Bhāgavata. Among those who are the votaries of the Kṛṣṇa cult, this hymn is very popular, and is on the lips of all ardent devotees. Being couched in the language of a love lyric, the philosophy behind it, and of the Bhāgavata in general, of which it is a wonderfully fragrant flower, requires some explanation for a general reader.

The Bhāgavata maintains that 'Kṛṣṇa is the Supreme Being Himself — Kṛṣṇastu bhagavān svayam.' It also maintains that God approaches man in the way man approaches Him. He can be approached, by those who prefer to do so, as the Almighty Impersonal Being, formless and all-pervading, who is the origin, sustentation and dissolving basis of the universe. But that formless Absolute, out of whom all forms have come, is also the Archetype of all Forms, and He accepts adoration of all aspirants, through all forms of human sentiments which make the mind absolutely concentrated on Him, whatever might be the motive force behind. Thus God can be approached through antagonism and fear as also through all forms of human love. As examples of approach through antagonism — *Vidveṣa-bhakti* — we are given in the Purāṇas the examples of Hiraṇyākṣa, Hiraṇyakaśipu, Rāvaṇa, Kaṁsa, Śiśupāla etc. The psychological principle behind this is that absolute antagonism and dread of God can make the mind concentrated on, and absorbed in Him and that He approaches such devotees as an antagonist with weapon in hand, which is the appropriate way of blessing such devotees. For confrontation with Him and death at His hand ultimately confer on them unity with Him. Such examples are however rare, and we read of them only in Purāṇas.

He is approachable through all forms of human love too, but we have first described devotion of the confrontation type, because it brings out clearly the truth that it is concentration and absorption of the mind in Him that accomplishes the transformation. It is this factor in human love devoted towards God that transforms the devotee too. Thus the Bhāgavata describes, besides Bhakti in the ordinary sense, i.e. as adoration of Him as the Supreme Being maintaining an attitude of awe and resignation along with desire for salvation, various other forms of love of Him as one's 'own' in a human sense — as one's Master, as one's child, as one's comrade and as one's husband and lover. In all these forms of love what is to be noticed is the intensity of it and the whole-hearted concentration on Him it begets, without forgetfulness of His cosmic aspect.

The Gopī-Kṛṣṇa episode, which is considered as the expression of the deepest longing of the human soul for the Supreme Being, is couched in the langauge of human love between a man and a woman, and is therefore likely to be mistaken by those, who are not acquainted with the Bhāgavata philosophy, as mere erotic poetry. It is not so. It is the longing of a pure soul for God as one's 'own'. This brief introduction to this great hymn, the Gopikā-gītam, is given to present the correct background to readers who are not acquainted with the Bhāgavata philosophy.]

*1*

जयति तेऽधिकं जन्मना व्रजः श्रयत इन्दिरा शश्वदत्र हि ।
दयित दृश्यतां दिक्षु तावकाः त्वयि धृतासवस्त्वां विचिन्वते ॥

*Jayati te'dhikam janmanā vrajaḥ*
*śrayata Indirā śaśvad atra hi* |
*dayita dṛśytām dikṣu tāvakāḥ*
*tvayi dhṛt āsavas tvām vicinvate* ||

By Thy birth all-round prosperity reigns in Vraja;
For, Lakṣmi, the Goddess of Prosperity and Plenty, resides here always to be in attendance on Thee.
O Dear One, we (the Gopi s) whose very life is centred in Thee
Are searching for Thee in anguish.
O Lord! Tarry not to come before our vision.

*2*

शरदुदाशये साधुजातसत् - सरसिजोदरश्रीमुषा दृशा ।
सुरतनाथ तेऽशुल्कदासिका वरद निघ्नतो नेह किं वधः ॥

*Śarad udāśaye sādhu jāta sat-*
*sarasij' odara śrīmuṣā dṛśā |*
*surata-nātha te' śulka-dāsikā*
*varada nighnato n'eha kim vadhaḥ ||*

O Lord of Cupid's Realm! O Boon-giver! Is it not slaughter on Thy part to strike us,
Thy servitors unbought, by the shaft of Thy looks,
Whose glory puts to shame the charm of autumn's lotus blooms.
O Lord, Tarry not to come before our vision.

*3*

विषजलाप्ययाद् व्यालराक्षसाद् वर्षमारुताद् वैद्युतानलात् ।
वृषमयात्मजाद् विश्वतोभयाद् ऋषभ ते वयं रक्षिता मुहुः ॥

*Viṣajal'āpyayād vyāla-rākṣasād*
*varṣa-mārutād vaidyut'ānalāt |*
*vṛṣamayātmajād viśvato-bhayād*
*ṛṣabha te vayam rakṣitā muhuḥ ||*

O Great Leader, from death by Kaliya's poison,
From the grip of the python-shaped demon,
From the destruction wrought by torrential rain, wind and lightning,
From dangerous demons like Agha and Vyoma —
From all such fears Thou didst protect us.
O Lord, Tarry not to come before our vision.

*4*

न खलु गोपिकानन्दनो भवान - खिलदेहिनामन्तरात्मदृक् ।
विखनसार्थितो विश्वगुप्तये सख उदेयिवान् सात्वतां कुले ॥

*Na khalu gopikā-nandano bhavān-*
*akhila-dehinām antar-ātma-dṛk* |
*vikhanas'ārthito viśva-guptaye*
*sakha udeyivān sātvatām kule* |

O Comrade! Thou art not merely the Gopikā's son,
But the witness of the inner essence of all embodied beings.
Prayed to by Brahmā, Thou hast dawned like the sun
On the clan of the Yadus for the protection of the worlds.
O Lord! Tarry not to come before our vision.

*5*

विरचिताभयं वृष्णिधुर्य ते चरणमीयुषां संसृतेर्भयात् ।
करसरोरुहं कान्त कामदं शिरसि धेहि नः श्रीकरग्रहम् ॥

*Viracit'ābhayam vṛṣṇi-dhurya te*
*caraṇam īyuṣām samsṛter bhayāt*
*kara-saroruham kānta kāmadaṁ*
*śirasi dhehi naḥ śrī-kara-graham* ||

O the greatest of Yadu's Clan! O Charmer of our hearts!

Place that comely hand of Thine on our head —
The hand that gives protection from Saṁsāra to those who seek refuge at Thy feet,
Which grants all boons to devotees,
And which held in wedlock the hand of Śrī.
O Lord, Tarry not to come before our vision!

*6*

व्रजजनार्तिहन् वीर योषितां निजजनस्मयध्वंसनस्मित ।
भज सखे भवत्किङ्करीः स्म नो जलरुहाननं चारु दर्शय ॥

*Vraja-jan'ārtihan vīra yoṣitāṁ*
*nija-jana-smaya-dhvaṁsana-smita* |
*bhaja sakhe bhavat-kiṅkarīḥ sma no*
*jalaruh'ānanam cāru darśaya* ||

O the Saviour of Vraja from all dangers!
O Hero! whose smile humbles the pride and unsettles the resolution
Of people like us who consider Thee as our own,
Come, O Comrade, to us who are Thy hand-maids,
And reveal to us, women, Thy most handsome face.
O Lord! Tarry not to come before our vision!

*7*

प्रणतदेहिनां पापकर्शनं तृणचरानुगं श्रीनिकेतनम् ।
फणिफणार्पितं ते पदाम्बुजं कृणु कुचेषु नः कृन्धि हृच्छयम् ॥

*Praṇata-dehinām pāpa-karśanam*
*tṛṇa-car'ānugam śrī-niketanam* |
*phaṇi-phaṇ'ārpitam te pad'āmbujam*
*kṛṇu kuceṣu naḥ kṛndhi hṛcchayam* ||

Place on our breasts Thy hallowed feet and assuage our burning passion —
The feet that verily destroy the sins of all who prostrate before them,
The feet that pursue the foot-steps of grazing cows,
The feet that provide an abode for goddess Śrī,
The feet that graced the head of the serpent Kāliya.
O Lord! Tarry not to come before our vision.

*8*

मधुरया गिरा वल्गुवाक्यया बुधमनोज्ञया पुष्करेक्षण ।
विधिकरीरिमा वीर मुह्यती - रधरसीधुना ऽऽप्याययस्व नः ॥

*Madhurayā girā valgu-vākyayā*
*bhudha manojñāya puṣkarekṣaṇa* |
*vidhikarīr imā vīra muhyatīr-*
*adhara sīdhun'ā py'āyayasva naḥ* ||

O Lotus-eyed one! By Thy sweet speech couched in charming words, enjoyable even to the wise,
Thou hast infatuated us who are at Thy bidding.
Now rejuvenate us by the honey of Thy lips.
O Lord! Tarry not to come before our vision.

*9*

तव कथामृतं तप्तजीवनं कविभिरीडितं कल्मषापहम् ।
श्रवणमङ्गलं श्रीमदाततं भुवि गृणन्ति ते भूरिदा जना ॥

*Tava kath'āmṛtam tapta-jīvanam*
*kavibhir īḍitam kalmaṣ'āpaham* |
*śravaṇa-maṅgalam srīmad'ātatam*
*bhuvi gṛṇanti te bhūridā janā* ||

The nectar of Thy excellences revives the anguished spirit of man;
It effaces all sins while wise men bestow their praise on it and live contemplating on it.
To hear them is itself auspicious and peace-generating.
Those indeed are the real gift-makers who spread them far and wide.
O Lord! Tarry not to come before our vision.

*10*

प्रहसितं प्रिय प्रेमवीक्षणं विहरणं च ते ध्यानमङ्गलम् ।
रहसि संविदो या हृदिस्पृशः कुहक नो मनः क्षोभयन्ति हि ॥

*Prahasitam priya prema-vīkṣaṇam*
*viharaṇaṁ ca te dhyāna-maṅgalam* |
*rahasi saṁvido yā hṛdi-spṛśaḥ*
*kuhaka no manaḥ kṣobhayanti hi* ||

O Dear One! O deceptive Lover! Thy sweet smile and loving looks,
Thy meditation-worthy pastimes and Thy enchanting and loving prattle in privacy —
All these are exciting our minds in the extreme.
O Lord! Tarry not to come before our vision!

*11*

चलसि यद् व्रजाच्चारयन् पशून् नलिनसुन्दरं नाथ ते पदम् ।
शिलतृणाङ्कुरै सीदतीति नः कलिलतां मनः कान्त गच्छति ॥

*Calasi yad vrajāc cārayan paśūn*
*nalina-sundaram nātha te padam*
*śila-tṛṅ'āṅkurai sīdatīti naḥ*
*kalilatām manaḥ kānta gacchati* ||

When Thou, O Lord and sweet Lover, movest away from Vraja to tend cattle
Our minds are extremely worried thinking
That Thy lotus-like feet might get hurt by stones and sharp ends of thorny grass.
O Lord! Tarry not to come before our vision.

*12*

दिनपरिक्षये नीलकुन्तलै - र्वनरुहाननं ब्रिभ्रदावृतम् ।
घनरजस्वलं दर्शयन् मुहु - र्मनसि नः स्मरं वीर यच्छसि ॥

*Dina-parikṣaye nīla-kuntalair*
*vanaruh'ānanam bibhrad'āvṛtam* |
*ghana-rajasvalam darśayan muhur*
*manasi naḥ smaram vīra yacchasi*

O our Smart Lover! At even-tide as we see Thee return after tending the cattle day-long,
With Thy lotus face surrounded by dark locks, all smeared with dust,
Repeated waves of hot passion excite our minds.
O Lord! Tarry not to come before our vision.

*13*

प्रणतकामदं पद्मजार्चितं धरणिमण्डनं ध्येयमापदि ।
चरणपङ्कजं शन्तमं च ते रमण नः स्तनेष्वर्पयाधिहन् ॥

*Praṇata-kāmadam padmaj'ārcitam*
*dharaṇi-maṇḍanaṁ dhyeyam āpadi* |
*caraṇa-paṅkajaṁ śantamaṁ ca te*
*ramaṇa naḥ staneṣv'arpay'ādhi-han*

O Delighter of our Hearts! And O Healer of our Woes!
Place on our breasts those lotus feet of Thine —
The feet that are bounteous to worshippers,
The feet that lotus-born goddess Padmā adores,
The feet that are an ornament to the world,
The feet that form the one object to be meditated upon in times of danger,

The feet which offer instant peace to those who contact them.
O Lord! Tarry not to come before our vision.

*14*

सुरतवर्धनं शोकनाशनं स्वरितवेणुना सुष्ठु चुम्बितम् ।
इतररागविस्मारणं नृणां वितर वीर नस्तेऽधरामृतम् ॥

*Surata-vardhanam śoka-nāśanam*
*svarita-veṇunā suṣṭhu cumbitam* |
*itara-rāga-vismāraṇam nṛṇām*
*vitara vīra nas'te' dhar'āmṛtam* ||

O Hero of the Realm of Love! Give us a draught of Thy honeyed-lips —
The lips that enhance the delight of amorous indulgences,
The lips that remove all sorrows,
The lips that are firmly kissed by the resounding flute,
The lips that erase every other form of longing from the heart of man.
O Lord! Tarry not to come before our vision.

*15*

अटति यद् भवानह्नि काननं त्रुटिर्युगायते त्वामपश्यताम् ।
कुटिलकुन्तलं श्रीमुखं च ते जड उदीक्षतां पक्ष्मकृद् दृशाम् ॥

*Aṭati yad bhavān ahni kānanaṁ*
*truṭir yugāyate tvām apaśyatām* |
*kuṭila-kuntalam śrīmukham ca te*
*jaḍa udīkṣatām pakṣmakṛd dṛśām* ||

When Thou art moving about in the forest during day time
A moment looks like an age to us who arenot able to see Thee,
Whose face of enchanting beauty is framed in curly locks.
A fool indeed is the creator for having fitted eyelids to our eyes that are so anxious to see Thee,
Thus causing a moment's oblivion while they wink.
O Lord! Tarry not to come before our vision.

*16*

पतिसुतान्वय भ्रातृबान्धवा - नतिविलङ्घ्य तेऽन्त्यच्युतागताः ।
गतिविदस्तवोद्गीतमोहिताः कितव योषितः कस्त्यजेन्निशि ॥

*Pati-sut'ānvaya-bhrātṛ'bāndhavān*
*ativilaṅghya te'nty'acyut'āgatāḥ* |
*gatividas tavodgīta mohit'āḥ*
*kitava yoṣitaḥ kas tyajen niśi* ||

Drawn by the music of Thy flute with which Thou didst call us,
We have come to Thee, Imperishable Lord,
Without caring for our husbands, sons, brothers and relatives.

Who else but Thou, O Rogue, would abandon such
women as ourselves at this dead of night?
O Lord! Tarry not to come before our eyes.

*17*

रहसि संविदं हृच्छयोदयं प्रहसिताननं प्रेमवीक्षणम् ।
बृहदुरः श्रियो वीक्ष्य धाम ते मुहुरतिस्पृहा मुह्यते मनः ॥

*Rahasi saṁvidaṁ hṛcchay'odayam*
*prahasit'ānanam prema-vīkṣaṇam* |
*bṛhad-uraḥ śriyo vīkṣya dhāma te*
*muhur atispṛhā muhyate manaḥ* ||

Waves and waves of hot passion surge in our mind,
driving us to frenzy,
When we think of Thy amorous conversations in privacy,
Thy face lit with a comely smile,
Thy glances scattering love,
And Thy broad chest that forms the abode of Goddess Śrī.
O Lord! Tarry not to come before our eyes.

*18*

व्रजवनौकसां व्यक्तिरङ्ग ते वृजिनहन्त्र्यलं विश्वमङ्गलम् ।
त्यज मनाक् च नस्त्वत्स्पृहात्मनां स्वजनहृद्रुजां यन्निषूदनम् ॥

*Vraja-van'aukasām vyaktir aṅga te*
*vṛjinahantry alam viśva-maṅgalam* |
*tyaja manāk ca nas tvat-spṛh'ātmanām*
*svajana-hṛdrujām yan niṣūdanam*

Thy assumption of an individuality is for the good of the world at large,
And specially for erasing the difficulties of the people of Vraja.
Therefore release without miserliness a little at least of that medicine well-known to Thee
To cure the ailment of the hearts of us who love Thee whole-heartedly.
O Lord! Tarry not to come before our eyes.

## *19*

यत्ते सुजातचरणाम्बुरुहं स्तनेषु भीताः शनैः प्रिय दधीमहि कर्कशेषु ।
तेनाटवीमटसि तद् व्यथते न किंस्वित् कूर्पादिभिर्भ्रमति धीर्भवदायुषां नः ॥

*Yat te sujāta caraṇ'āmbu-ruham staneṣu*
*bhītāḥ śanaiḥ priya dadhīmahi karkaśeṣu* |
*ten'āṭavīm aṭasi tad vyathate na kiṁsvit*
*kūrpādibhir bhramati dhīr bhavad-āyuṣām naḥ* ||

O Dearest One! We hold Thy tender feet only very gently and cautiously to our hard breasts.
We who live only for Thy sake are therefore very anxious to think

That those feet, to be thus held and protected,
Are being painfully lacerated by walking over stones and thorns in the forest.
O Lord! Tarry not to come before our vision!

*20*

इति गोप्यः प्रगायन्त्यः प्रलपन्त्यश्च चित्रधा ।
रुरुदुः सुस्वरं राजन् कृष्णदर्शनलालसाः ॥

*Iti gopyaḥ pragāyantyaḥ pralapantyaś ca citradhā*
*ruruduḥ susvaram rājan kṛṣṇa-darśana lālasāḥ*

Thus, O King, did the Gopīkās wail at the top of their voice,
Singing and raving in their intense longing to meet Kṛṣṇa.

*21*

तासामाविरभूच्छौरिः स्मयमानमुखाम्बुजः ।
पीताम्बरधरः स्रग्वी साक्षान्मन्मथमन्मथः ॥

*Tāsām āvirabhūc chauriḥ smayamāna mukh'āmbujaḥ* |
*pītāmbara-dharaḥ sragvī sākṣān manmatha manmathaḥ* ||

To them Kṛṣṇa now reappeared suddenly with a smiling face,
Dressed in yellow silk and wearing a wreath of flowers,
In a form that would infatuate Cupid himself.